Business E-Mail

"A lot of employers (and job-hunters) I know are being driven nuts by their e-mail. From a nifty little utility a few years back, e-mail has evolved into a monster that threatens to take over our whole lives. Lisa Smith knows the rules that can enable us to tame the monster and harness the true potential of e-mail. Strange rules, sometimes, like: why you shouldn't begin a sentence or paragraph in e-mail with the word 'From'. I highly recommend this little book; we all need its wisdom."

—Richard N. Bolles

Author, *What Color Is Your Parachute? A Practical Manual for Job-Hunters & Career-Changers*
Completely rewritten in 2002

Business E-Mail

How to Make It Professional and Effective

Lisa A. Smith

Dec. 2006

Writing & Editing at Work™

San Anselmo, California

Writing & Editing at Work
PO Box 2543
San Anselmo, CA 94979

www.writingandeditingatwork.com
admin@writingandeditingatwork.com

Publisher's Cataloging-in-Publication Data
Smith, Lisa A.
    Business e-mail : how to make it professional and
effective / Lisa A. Smith. -- 1st ed.
       p. cm.
    Includes bibliographical references and index.
    LCCN 2002100703
    ISBN 0-9709513-2-9

    1. Business writing--Data processing. 2. Electronic
mail messages. 3. English language--Business English.
I. Title.

HF5718.3.S65 2002   808'.06665
                         QB102-200189

Printed in the United States of America on acid-free paper

Special Sales
Discounts are available on bulk purchases for special markets or
premium use. For more information, contact
admin@writingandeditingatwork.com.

Contents

Part 1: How to make e-mail work for you

Introduction

From worldwide conglomerates to one-person companies in home offices, all businesses can profit from using e-mail in a professional way.

As individuals, we enjoy the advantages of using e-mail: less printing of letters and envelopes, less money spent on postage, fewer interruptions caused by phone calls. And e-mail is so easy to use, so available, that we don't think twice about sending message after message.

No wonder our e-mail inboxes are full – both at the office and at home. Staying in touch with friends and family has never been easier. You probably don't want to slow down your personal e-mail by thinking about spelling, punctuation, grammar, or any other aspect of more formal writing. But on the job – in messages sent within your company and those sent to outsiders – e-mail takes on another dimension.

Whether you're writing a thank-you note to a client, an invitation to a lunch honoring a co-worker, a reminder about a department meeting, an announcement about your company's participation in a volunteer project, a proposal, a request for a quote, or a direct sales pitch, your e-mail message represents your business.

Because every line you write is a marketing tool™ you want to be sure that your e-mail presents your company in a positive way. What you say – and how you say it – affects the image of your company. It also affects what people in the business world think about you. And it can have a profound effect on your company's bottom line.

So what image of your company and yourself do you want to project through your e-mail messages? My guess is that you'd like people to think of your company as being responsive to their needs, knowledgeable about their problems, considerate of their schedules and deadlines, and adaptable to their changing requirements. And you'd want them to think of you as a caring and careful professional.

The guidelines presented in this book will help you use e-mail in ways that present you and your company in a positive light. You'll learn why it's important to make sure that every business-related e-mail message you send is

- necessary
- appropriate for the medium
- within company guidelines
- clear and well written
- error free
- brief and to the point

Everything I've just said applies to interoffice messages as well as those to the outside world. It's in your best interest to present the same positive image of yourself to co-workers, subordinates, and managers as you do to outside colleagues, suppliers, customers, and clients. Furthermore, if you are careful about the e-mail you send to co-workers, you may help to reduce their stress on the job.

Research by Christina A. Cavanagh, a professor of management communications at The University of Western Ontario, shows that "the major cause of e-mail stress in the workplace is in its inappropriate use as a communication tool, not its volume" and that e-mail "is better suited to certain types of information exchange than others." Also, Cavanagh asked research participants to describe what they considered to be poorly written e-mail. From their responses, she concluded that e-mail messages "are heavily judged on their professional appearance and the care taken in their construction."

The purpose of this book is to show you how to make your e-mail messages work for you rather than against you in the business world. Well-written e-mail that looks and sounds professional makes it easier for clients, customers, and co-workers to do business with you and helps them feel good about your company and you. Follow the guidelines presented and you will improve your reputation as a thoughtful communicator whose e-mail messages are welcomed, opened, understood, and answered.

The first four chapters end with a one-page summary – a bare-bones outline or cheat sheet related to the text. You may copy those pages and post them at your computer workstation. Use them to jog your memory about the most important points you need to follow when composing, sending, and replying to business-related e-mail.

Using e-mail professionally

What if e-mail didn't exist? (I know it's hard to imagine, but humor me for just a moment.) Would you need to communicate the content of your intended e-mail message in some other medium right now? Would you phone or fax or write a letter right now? Or would you wait until you had more to say? Or until you ran into the intended recipient in the hall or at lunch? Does the recipient really need to see your message right now? Is the information crucial? If your message can be easily postponed, or if it doesn't have a specific business-related purpose, then perhaps it doesn't need to be sent at all.

Obviously, if your company's policy precludes the sending and receiving of personal messages during work hours or on company equipment, then personal e-mail would be considered unnecessary.

And just because a message is work related doesn't mean it necessarily has to be sent via e-mail. Think of e-mail within your company as an interoffice memo. Would you really need to send a memo to every employee on the company list, whether they work inhouse or not, to announce that you were going to be away from your desk for a short while? Or would you just tell a co-worker at a nearby desk?

Andrea Zuercher, a telecommuter from Kansas, said, "It's of no use to me whatsoever to know that Employee A back at the main office in Maryland is going out on a brief errand. A significant absence, yes – it's useful to know that, in case I need something fast and can't get an answer. But a quick dash to the bathroom or the ATM? No, I don't need to know about it."

Before clicking the Send button, ask yourself if everyone you're sending the message to really needs to receive it.

Will your e-mail messages be welcome?
Just because e-mail may be your favorite method of business communication, don't assume that everyone else feels the same way. Now that e-mail has become ubiquitous as a means of business communication, some busy people may prefer not to be interrupted by it throughout the workday. Instead, they let incoming messages accumulate, and take care of them just once or twice each day. In some offices, therefore, your messages may receive more attention and faster responses if they're sent by fax.

Don't count on e-mail as a means of handling urgent business unless you know the recipients' e-mail habits or you have alerted them – by some other means of communication – that your e-mail message is on its way.

Be especially cautious about sending unsolicited e-mail to people outside of the company or above you in the corporate hierarchy. The best way to find out their communication preferences is to ask them – using a medium other than e-mail. If necessary, write their names on a list with four columns (e-mail, phone, fax, US mail) to help you remember and respect their wishes.

If one of your tasks is to send out press releases, you'll want to find out how particular reporters and other media representatives prefer to receive them. Some want to get hard copy first, with follow-up via e-mail. Others prefer e-mail first, with phoned follow-up. And still others think e-mail works best all around.

You may also find that many independent contractors, professionals, CEOs, owners of small businesses, and others whose work lives are not constrained by regular days and hours prefer e-mail communication because they can tend to it from any place and at any time of day or night.

Business-related e-mail correspondence initiated by someone unknown to you and outside of your company – a potential client, customer, vendor, or service provider, for example – can safely be answered by e-mail, if only to acknowledge receipt of the message. Whether you respond to the content itself via e-mail, by phone, or on your letterhead will depend on the nature of the received message and on whether an e-mail response is appropriate and within company policy.

Will the joke be on you?

Consider the people you're writing to. Will they be glad to find a list of jokes in their inbox? Or will they think of it as an annoyance to be deleted without reading? Even worse, will they feel that they have to take the time to respond not because they want to but because courtesy demands a response? A freelance editor on the East Coast, who chooses to remain anonymous for obvious reasons, said, "I am not pleased with business contacts who send long lists of forwarded jokes as attachments. I feel obliged to open them, read them, and comment on them, although I'd rather not."

One of my colleagues regularly sends humorous e-mail to a long list of business associates. When she started, she asked everyone on her list to let her know if they wanted to be taken off. Some people enjoy the diversion of a little humor in the middle of the workday. Others find it intrusive, especially when the same old jokes make the rounds again and again.

Humor can backfire in other ways. People may resent jokes that poke fun at their religious or political beliefs. Of course those topics are best avoided in business communications anyway, unless you're absolutely certain that your readers share your beliefs. Humor that plays on sexual orientation or race does not belong in a business environment.

When I asked a group of editors to tell me their pet peeves about e-mail at work, the annoyance mentioned most often was receiving endlessly forwarded lists of jokes, false virus alerts, scams, hoaxes, urban legends, and petitions about political and social issues. Busy professionals don't appreciate having to take the time to clear such messages out of their mailboxes at work.

Why would you send false messages to your friends and business associates? If you're tempted to forward virus alerts, scams, hoaxes, and legends, spend a couple of minutes on the Web to check their veracity; you'll probably find out that they are false and not worthy of being perpetuated. (Hint: Go to your favorite search engine and type in "scam" or "urban legend".) If your company has an IT (Information Technology) or MIS (Management Information Systems) department, send virus alerts there; the specialists in those departments know how to handle them.

Get permission

Before sending any e-mail that does not focus strictly on business, either within or outside your company, consider asking permission of the recipient. You may find out, for example, that a colleague across town does not appreciate receiving industry gossip via e-mail because of privacy concerns, or that a co-worker two floors up deletes anything trivial without even opening it.

If you think there is the slightest chance your e-mail might be thought of as an imposition, don't send it.

Attachments

Your company may have a policy about sending and receiving attachments. Always get permission before sending an attachment to someone outside or within your company for the first time. Attachments can carry destructive or disruptive viruses and worms. If you had opened an attachment carrying the infamous love bug virus, for example, it would have copied your address book and sent the same corrupted file to everyone on your list, making it appear as if the message had come from you.

So, despite the fact that most people now have anti-virus software, if you want to be sure your attachments are welcome, it's a good idea to ask first every time. Most people won't open attachments from strangers, even if they appear to come from reputable corporations. And wise people won't open attachments from people they do know, unless they've been told to expect them.

Another reason not to send an attachment without permission is that it may be rejected even before it reaches its intended target. As communications director for a software company and co-host of the radio program Technology Corner on WTVN in Columbus, Ohio, Bill Blinn knows about such things. He said, "In most cases, I don't mind receiving large attachments as long as I know in advance that they're coming, and the person sends them to me at an address where they'll be accepted. For example, my Roadrunner account will accept no more than 10MB, and I think the largest single file can be only 5MB. I ask people to send large files to a special account at blinn.com. Of course there are better ways to get a large file from one person to another – FTP or Xdrive, for example – and e-mail should be the last resort if the person you're sending the file to didn't specifically request that you e-mail it."

Unless formatting is important, short files don't need to be sent as attachments; they can simply be copied and pasted into the body of an e-mail message.

Finally, there is the matter of downloading time. Not everyone can take advantage of high-speed cable, DSL, or network connections. Business travelers may have to use slow phone connections in out-of-the-way hotels; independent contractors, telecommuters, and others may work in rural areas or terrain where fast connections are not available. And many who work in big cities still use standard – meaning "snail-like" compared to the high-speed variety – Internet connections.

For those people, downloading large uncompressed attachments – especially those with graphics – can be excruciatingly slow, which is another important reason not to attach anything that's not related to business.

Kelly Wright, an editor in Chicago, said, "My office has a speedy T1 line, but I also work at home, where my standard dial-up connection is pretty slow. Once my computer starts downloading a large file, there's no stopping it: I'm stuck for half an hour, waiting to receive some picture I never wanted anyway. When I do need graphics files for a project, I ask clients to compress them with WinZip or another such compression utility before sending them to me."

Does your message fit the medium?

E-mail often feels like face-to-face conversation; it's usually short, snappy, and to the point. But in brief, quickly written messages, it's difficult to convey the clues to meaning that are inherent in tone of voice, facial expression, and body language. Sarcasm and irony, for example, can't be readily expressed in e-mail. And emoticons or symbols like ;-) and : (don't usually fit the formality of business communications.

Without clear signals about the attitude behind your words, recipients might misconstrue your meaning. Ambiguities can arise where none were intended. When you need to discuss sensitive matters – trade secrets, job performance, or hiring and firing, for example – it might be better to choose another medium for your message. A long, well-thought-out, and carefully worded letter (which, of course, can be sent by e-mail, if privacy is not a concern) or a one-to-one talk is less likely to result in misunderstanding.

How do you know whether e-mail is the appropriate medium to use for a particular business communication? You wouldn't ask that question about snail mail, so why question the appropriateness of e-mail? Because e-mail differs from regular mail in at least three significant ways.

Privacy. You never know who's going to read the e-mail messages you send. Even if you send a message to someone who lives alone and works in his or her home office, if the computers in *your* workplace are on a network, then someone else could read what you've sent. Become familiar with your company's policy regarding the monitoring of employee e-mail and Internet use. Find out what sort of e-mail the company does not condone. Jobs have been lost and lives have been ruined because workers either did not know or chose to disregard company policy on this matter.

If the information you need to communicate about is confidential, and there is a possibility that someone other than you and the recipient could read your message, then e-mail might not be an appropriate medium.

Confidentiality may be an important aspect of your work. If that is the case, and you need to send frequent confidential e-mail, then you probably need an encryption program. Ask your computer network administrator or technician about what is available.

Would it be all right with you if someone quoted what you have written? (Not that they should without your permission, of course.) Might your words hurt someone? If your message fell into the wrong hands, if it became public, might it be considered libelous? Is it possible that your message might be considered an act of harassment? Is there a chance you and your company could be sued? Would you care if the boss – or your mother – read your message?

Remember: E-mail is not private – and messages do not completely disappear just because you have deleted them from your e-mail program at the office.

Legality. If you don't yet have access to electronic signature software, and you want to send, via e-mail, a contract, proposal, quote, or other message that requires signatures, then you will also need to send it via fax or regular mail. You'd probably want to do that anyway, so that the document and signatures would appear on your company letterhead. In any case, be sure to check with your corporate counsel about the legality of such documents if sent by e-mail.

Direct mail marketing through the post office can result in lucrative sales. And it's legal. Sending legitimate but unsolicited marketing pieces to a long list of recipients via e-mail may also be legal. But it is spam, and it can result in loss of good will and loss of service by your company's ISP. Before sending any material that contains advertising to a list of e-mail addresses, be sure that each addressee has opted in to your list. Newsletters can be excellent promotional tools, but don't distribute your business newsletter via e-mail to anyone who has not signed up to receive it.

Keeping a paper trail that can serve as evidence in the event of disputes is a wise precaution; it may even be part of your company's policy. If not, at least consider printing out and saving e-mail (both sent and received) that pertains to bids, quotes, orders, deliveries, disagreements, invoices, payments, promises, contracts, and other legal matters.

Another matter of legality involves copyright. Whoever writes a letter or message of any sort owns the copyright to it, just as if it were a book. A business owns the copyright to material printed on its letterhead. You may own the hard copy of the letter sent to you via the post office, but you are not entitled to reproduce it or distribute it to others without the copyright owner's permission. The same goes for e-mail messages. This means that you do not have the right to forward private messages that come from outside your company without permission of the original sender. You also do not have the right to copy material from Web sites and send it to others without permission of the site's copyright holder. Check with your company counsel about copyright matters.

➤ Remember: Don't forward copyrighted messages without permission.

Formality. The formality of messages sent on company letterhead is probably more appropriate than e-mail for certain other communications as well. Letters of recommendation, for example, might be more impressive on letterhead than on e-mail. Nonprofit groups would probably be wise to send requests for donations or announcements of fund drives on organization letterhead. Messages that recipients are likely to want to save or, perhaps, frame – congratulatory letters, notifications of prestigious acceptance or awards – should be mailed on letterhead, although early notice may be sent via e-mail.

Remember the human touch

Recently I sent an e-mail requesting a quote from a service bureau I had not used before. The company replied with a well-written thank-you-for-the-opportunity-to-bid note; beneath the signature was the information I had asked for. Later that day I e-mailed revised specs to the same company and asked for another quote. An hour later I received the same well-written note followed by a quote. At first I thought some glitch in cyberspace had caused the service bureau's first response to be resent. But when I looked more closely at the numbers, I realized they represented the revised quote. I did not appreciate receiving that canned message twice in one day.

Clients feel depersonalized when they realize you are serving them with templates. In the situation I just described, one short line (Here is the revised quote you requested.) would have prevented depersonalization, taken up less bandwidth, and let me know that someone was tending to my needs. It pays to pay attention to such details; they generate goodwill by pleasing clients and customers.

Keep it short and sweet

Developing a reputation as someone who writes clear, direct, and concise e-mail messages will certainly help you in the business world. Clarity and brevity save time. Recipients of your e-mail will appreciate your efforts to help them save time. Limit each message to just one topic. Know the purpose of your message and make that purpose clear in as few words as possible. If your purpose is to give information, ask recipients to print or save the message as a reference. If you need or want a response, ask for it. If no response is necessary, say so.

Your reputation will also be enhanced by courtesy, warmth, and appropriate humor – none of which need take up too much of your time. You can add commonly used phrases like "Thank you" and "Best wishes" and "How thoughtful of you" to the AutoText list in your word processing program. And one-liners can be just as funny as long, drawn-out stories. You might collect twelve one-liners or short quotations that pertain to your business or profession and use them as part of your e-mail signature, changing them monthly.

E-mail lists

Like many workers, whether on staff or contract, you probably belong to at least one e-mail discussion list that relates to your work. These lists may offer the latest information in a particular field, immediate answers to work-related questions, peer support, and a feeling of community among colleagues throughout the United States and the world.

When you join a list, you receive a welcome message that contains guidelines for participation and instructions for managing your subscription. Read and save that message! If you don't, you risk embarrassing yourself or your company.

Guidelines for most e-mail discussion lists ask that self-promotion be limited to a signature file of no more than four to six lines. You don't have to use a signature file, but you do need to sign your name. Not adding your name to a list message is just plain rude, especially when your e-mail address is different from your own name. Why should anyone give credence to a message that appears to be sent anonymously? Monitored lists usually prohibit attachments, flames, and spam. And all guidelines give instructions telling you how to unsubscribe; sending an unsubscribe message to the list itself is not the way to do it and is one sure way to annoy other list members.

Ruth E. Thaler-Carter, a freelance writer and editor in Rochester, New York, said, "People who don't bother to read the guidelines before participating in lists irk me with their unprofessional and unbusinesslike behavior. They send messages that are irrelevant (off-topic or personal rather than list-oriented) or inappropriately formatted (incomplete, without subject tags, or without signatures), or they use the list for blatant self-promotion. There's a thin line between letting colleagues know who you are and what you do and baldly advertising your professional services."

If you work in a large company or organization, you're probably on an inhouse e-mail list. A major problem with house lists is that information pertinent only to particular subgroups within the company may be sent to all employees by mistake or because subgroups have not been created in the e-mail program. Everyone may be interested in knowing, for example, the date of the company picnic; but only those who work in production need to know when their department meeting will be held. If departmental or other special mail lists exist within your company, be sure to use them when appropriate. If those lists would be useful but don't yet exist, do what you can to have them created.

Sarah Bane, a technical writer and instructor in Fort Smith, Arkansas, said, "At the college where I teach evening classes, e-mail is replacing paper memos as the primary means of communication. Apparently no one has bothered setting up separate mailing lists for full-time and part-time employees. Consequently, we part-timers receive numerous e-mails about benefits for which we are not eligible or meetings in which we have no voice. I see no reason these should take up space in our e-mailboxes." Clearly, in this case, a full-time employee in administration should be responsible for creating and maintaining a special mail list for part-time instructors.

Good manners are good for your career. List etiquette, like all manners, involves thoughtfulness and consideration of others. Here are four more tips on list behavior:

- Unless a survey has been asked for, avoid "me too" replies; they take up bandwidth and don't add substance to the discussion.
- Think before clicking on "Reply All." Does your response really need to go to the whole list, or would a private reply be more appropriate?
- Replies may be needlessly long if your e-mail preferences are set to include the original message in your reply; the "original message" may contain an entire thread! Cut, cut, cut. Leave only what readers will need to understand your reply.
- If you're going to be away from your computer for several days or weeks, notify the list server to set your account to "postpone" or "no mail."

Handling e-mail efficiently
People generally expect to receive answers to e-mailed business questions quickly – certainly within 24 hours. If

they don't hear from you within that time, they might contact a competitor. If, for some good reason, you can't give them the information they want quickly, the smart and courteous thing to do is to thank them for contacting you, let them know that you're working on their request, and tell them when they can expect a complete answer.

When you go on vacation or on a business trip that will keep you away from the office for more than a day or so, you can arrange to have an automatic response sent to all the e-mail that arrives during your absence.

Here's a sample message for an automatic response that provides the kind of information clients, customers, and co-workers need to know:

> Tracy Playgirl will be away from the office from 4/2 through 4/5. If you need an immediate response, please contact Melissa Stalwart at mstalwart@mycompany.com or phone 800-555-4567, ext. 89.

Some e-mail programs offer auto-response as an option or "out of office" tool. If you don't find such an option in your program, check with someone in your company's IT or MIS department. If your company doesn't have an IT department or your e-mail program doesn't offer an auto-response option, perhaps you could switch to a program that does.

When you do set up an auto-response system for your e-mail, be sure that the automatic replies don't get sent in response to messages that come through e-mail discussion lists; they could flood the lists and annoy all the other participants, who would receive multiple copies throughout the time you are away. (That's one good reason to set your list accounts to "postpone" or "no mail" before you leave.)

Make a list and check it twice

The criteria you use to determine if your e-mail messages are necessary, appropriate, and appreciated by recipients will depend partly on the position you hold, the work functions you perform, and the policies already set by your company. If no such policies exist, you can create your own list of criteria based on what you learn from this book, or copy the list of questions on the next page. Perhaps the most important question is whether e-mail will be the most effective medium in which to communicate a particular message to a particular recipient.

It's quicker, easier, less painful, and more considerate to check a message against a list of criteria before you send it than to apologize for mistakes or repair damage later. Ralph Waldo Emerson wrote, "I wish to say what I think and feel today, with the proviso that tomorrow perhaps I shall contradict it all." Sounds to me like wishful thinking when applied to the business world of the twenty-first century. You may not be able to afford the luxury of contradicting your statements tomorrow, so think before you click "Send."

(Copy this page and post it at your workstation for easy reference.)

Using e-mail professionally

- Is this message related to business?
- Is the information important enough to send?
- Does everyone in the To, CC, and BCC fields need to see this message?
- Does the message contain references to religion, politics, sexual orientation, or race?
- If you're forwarding a message, have you checked it for hoaxes, scams, urban legends, or false virus alerts?
- Might recipients think of this message as an imposition on their time?
- If your message is urgent, are you sure the recipient will read it immediately?
- Do the addressees welcome e-mail messages?
- Do you have the addressees' permission to send e-mail to them?
- If you have attached a file, do you have permission from the addressee to do so?
- Is the attachment necessary and related to business?
- Would anyone mind if the content of this message became public knowledge?
- Do you have permission to forward a copyrighted message?
- Is the purpose of your message clear?
- Does your message conform to company policy and list rules?
- Is e-mail the most effective way to communicate this particular message to this particular recipient?

From *Business E-Mail: How to Make It Professional and Effective*
© 2002 by Lisa A. Smith

Formatting e-mail

When you send a letter or fax on company letterhead, you know that the recipient will see it exactly the way you sent it, with all formatting intact. Tables and tabbed lists will maintain their integrity; words typed in italics or bold will remain italicized or bold. But when you send a message out into the ether, you lose control over how it will appear when it arrives at its destination.

Here's a test you can run if you want to see for yourself what happens when a carefully crafted missile is shot into cyberspace. Find three people who use different e-mail programs on Macs and three who use different e-mail programs on PCs. Ask them to help you test your e-mail system. Then type the following message into your word processing program; format it with numbering for the list of questions, with tabs for the list of dates, and with the same line length that you see here.

> This is a test of my e-mail system. Please print out this message and fax it to me at 555-123-4567. Also, please be sure that your reply options are set to include the original message before you reply to the questions below.
>
> 1. Does this URL <writing-at-work.com> appear as a link in your screen?
> 2. How about this one? www.writing-at-work.com
> 3. And this one? http://www.writing-at-work.com
> 4. Is this book title, *Moby Dick,* italicized?
> 5. What number follows this question? ½
> In the list that follows, note the tabbed spacing:
> 2001   Nov.   Jan.   Aug.   Apr.
> 2002   Nov.   Dec.   Jan.   Feb.
> 2003   Aug.   Oct.   Nov.   Dec.
> Thank you for taking part in this test.

Copy and paste the message into your e-mail program, and send it to the six people who agreed to participate. I'll bet your e-mail doesn't look the same on all six faxes you receive from them. I'll bet you won't get the same answers to your questions from all six people. And I'll bet your original doesn't look the same on all six replies.

What follows is how distorted the message looked when sent from AOL on one PC to ATTBI on another PC:

> This is a test of my e-mail system. Please print outthis message and fax it to me at 555-123-4567. Also,

please be sure that yourreply options are set to include the original message before you reply to thequestions below. I.

Does this URL<writing-at-work.com> appear as a link on your screen?2.

How about this one? www.writing-at-work.com3.

And

this one? http://www.writing-at-work.com4.Is this

book title, *MobyDick*, italicized?5.   What

number followsthis question? ½

In the list that follows, note the tabbed spacing: 2001

Nov.	Jan.		Aug.	Apr.	
	2002	Nov.	Dec.	Jan.Feb.	
2003	Aug.		Oct.	Nov.	Dec.

Thank you for taking part in this test.

When sent from ATTBI on a PC to Earthlink on a Mac, the message was not quite as mangled, perhaps because Outlook Express was used on both. The misalignments are only mildly disconcerting; but a big problem is that the fraction "½" came across as "1Z2," which could lead to confusion, misunderstanding, or worse:

This is a test of my e-mail system. Please print out this message and
fax it to me at 555-123-4567. Also, please be sure that

your reply options are set to include the original message before you reply to the questions below.

1. Does this URL <writing-at-work.com> appear as a link in your screen?

2. How about this one? www.writing-at-work.com

3. And this one? http://www.writing-at-work.com

4. Is this book title, Moby Dick, italicized?

5. What number follows this question? 1Z2

In the list that follows, note the tabbed spacing:

2001 Jan. Feb. Aug. Oct.

2002 Nov. Dec. Jan. Feb.

2003 Aug. Oct. Nov. Dec.

Thank you for taking part in this test.

So, does this mean you don't need to think about formatting when writing e-mail? Sorry. No, it doesn't. In fact it means you need to think all the more carefully about formatting to make sure that your business messages will make sense and be easily understood no matter what e-mail program or computer they're read on.

Setting format options

Every e-mail program is different. If you check the drop-down menus in yours, you will most likely find one that allows you to set options or preferences for composing and sending e-mail. Your goal is to choose options that will cause the least trouble when your mail is received by other programs.

Text. Most e-mail programs allow you to choose between sending HTML (Hypertext Markup Language) and Plain Text. Choose Plain Text, also known as ASCII, for two reasons: (1) some of your recipients may have older e-mail programs that can't read HTML; and (2) unless certain precautions are taken, HTML mail can be bugged. Also, many work-related e-mail discussion groups do not accept HTML text.

First Lt. Willard Hughes, a former newspaper copy editor who is now an instructor in the California Cadet Corps, said emphatically, "E-mail should be sent in 'Plain Text' format. HTML, Rich Text Format, Virtual Business Cards, and so forth should not be sent until the sender has verified that the addressee is capable of receiving such and wants to do so. Unfortunately, the default setting in many e-mail programs nowadays is to send all outgoing mail in some fancy format. Users need to dig around in their Options, Tools, or Preferences boxes and summarily disable those features."

Encoding. Encoding changes messages and attachments from the format they're in when you send them (rtf, doc, jpg, and so forth) to plain text, which is all that can be transmitted over the Internet, and then back to their original format when they reach their destination. Three encoding methods exist: BinIIex, common for Macs; UUencode, originally used only on Unix computers; and MIME, which stands for "Multipurpose Internet Mail Extensions." If you must choose among them, pick MIME, which is the most recent and most common method for e-mail, although it won't work with all programs.

Line Length. One of my pet peeves is e-mail messages that arrive in my mailbox looking like this:

What would you call this phenomenon? Is it a

function of

particular

e-mail

programs?

Is it

something the sender can control? How can it

be prevented? What

should

people do to

make it stop?

Eleven lines instead of three. Eleven lines that are hard to read. Eleven double-spaced lines taking up so much space that I had to scroll down to read them all.

Bill Blinn, the Technology Corner radio host, explains the problem and gives a solution:

> The sender's lines are too long. Some programs treat e-mail like a word processor document: lines are not terminated and paragraphs are marked with one or more LF/CR (line feed/carriage return) pairs.
>
> When these programs send their messages, one of several events will happen: (1) The long lines will be sent as is, leaving it up to the receiver's e-mail program to resolve where the line breaks go. If this could be counted on to happen, everything would be fine. (2) The e-mail server – or some machine along the route – doesn't like long lines and inserts arbitrary returns. This usually works out fairly well. (3) The sending program may insert LF/CR every 100 characters or so,

meaning that you receive some normal-length lines, wrapped by your e-mail program, and some short lines, wrapped by the sender's program.

To solve the problem, every e-mail program should be set to wrap outgoing text at about the 75th character. That way messages will fit on 99.99% of the screens in use.

So, if the option exists in your e-mail program, set your text to wrap automatically at 65 to 75 characters, and you won't be guilty of adding to the problem.

Font settings. Business e-mail is not the place to get fancy with fonts. Once again, search your Options, Tools, or Preferences menus to find the boxes in which you can set your font choices. In Outlook Express for the PC, for example, click on Tools, then Options, and then on the Compose tab. You will be able to set fonts for mail and for news. Choose a common, easy-to-read font like Times New Roman or Arial. If you often send long messages, use a serif font (Times New Roman). Sans serif (Arial) is difficult to read except in short bursts. That's why books and newspapers use serif typefaces.

Even though your particular message may be short, your recipients may read it as one of 50 or 100 others. Make it easy on their eyes. Set your font in regular style and at a size large enough to be read both on screen and in printed form without a magnifying glass; 11 or 12 points works well for just about everybody. (What you are reading now is 11-point type.) Some e-mail programs don't allow you to set point size; instead they offer options like "Largest, Larger, Medium, Smaller, Smallest." Choose the one that is at least as large as the type in this book.

If you have the option of choosing a color, don't. Black is basic for business correspondence in any format. You can't go wrong with black; everyone will be able to read it. Colors show up differently on different monitors; some, like yellow, can be almost impossible to read on certain screens.

Formatting within your message

Now that you have set your options for simplicity and readability, continue to make things easy for your readers by avoiding everything but the most basic formatting within the messages you write.

On a PC, for example, any symbol created by holding down the ALT key and pressing a code on the numeric keypad (or by clicking on Insert and then Symbol) may not show up on your recipient's screen the way you intended it to. Remember how the fraction "½" showed up as "1Z2" when sent from a PC to a Mac, even though the e-mail program for both was Outlook Express? (The fraction was created on the sender's PC by holding down ALT and pressing 0189 on the numeric keypad.) Of course ½ looks more elegant than 1/2, and on hard copy you would certainly want to use the better-looking fractions. But when writing e-mail, stick to the clunkier-looking numbers or use decimals. Entering .5 instead of 1/2 is probably a good compromise and could avoid misunderstandings, especially if you're using mixed numbers like 2 1/2; it's much safer to type 2.5.

What if you're corresponding internationally? It would be polite to use your numeric keypad and insert accents or other diacritical marks when they appear in the names of people or places – the ö in Köln, for instance, the á in Juárez, or the ñ in Muñoz. But don't do it until you check with the addressees and conduct a test to see if their e-mail programs will interpret the symbol codes correctly. A missing diacritical mark would be less offensive than gibberish.

All the other fine points – dashes, bulleted or tabbed lists, indented paragraphs, italics, bold – that add class and subtlety to hard copy can cause trouble when inserted in e-mail messages because of the lack of standardization across platforms, programs, and ISPs.

You can work around some of them with ease. For example, instead of using **bold** for emphasis, insert asterisks before and after the *word or phrase* to be stressed. In hard copy you would type book titles like *Moby Dick* in italics; in e-mail use underscoring before and after the title, like this: _Little Women_. Use double spacing instead of indented lines to differentiate between paragraphs, white space makes the black type easier to read. Substitute double hyphens -- for dashes.

E-mail peculiarities

Some formatting problems have no equivalents in word-processing programs or hard copy. Nor are these problems found in all e-mail programs or on all servers, and therein lies the rub: you won't know whether something strange and unintended will appear in your message when it is received. But you can prevent at least three of these oddities.

Links. Certain e-mail programs, like older versions of Claris E-Mailer for the Mac, AOL 5.0 for the Mac, and AOL 6.0 for the PC, don't recognize URLs (Uniform Resource Locators or Web addresses) or e-mail addresses as links at all. The URLs you may see as blue links when you type them in show up in those programs as ordinary black type. One correspondent told me, "I'm using a fairly old version of CompuServe for my e-mail. I didn't upgrade to their web-type version because it dropped some options that I liked, so I don't see links or anything in color." Other programs, like Outlook Express 5.01 for Mac, will not show partial URLs as links; the http:// must be included.

For various reasons, many people continue to use old e-mail programs instead of upgrading to newer versions. Therefore it's best to write out your Internet address completely in your messages and in your signature file. In this way you'll know that all but the oldest programs will show your Web address as a link for readers to click on; users whose programs don't show links will at least be able to copy and paste the whole address into their browser's address field.

From. Another e-mail oddity involves the word "From." When you send a message that contains a line beginning with that word, with an uppercase "F," some e-mail programs display the word with an angle bracket (>) in front of it, as if it were part of a reply.

This peculiarity was pointed out by Mark L. Levinson, who at the time was a managing writer and editor for an Israeli data-security company. He said, "Sending e-mail from home (Netscape) to work (Outlook), I found that a lowercase 'from' was left alone at the start of a line, but an uppercase 'From' got the greater-than sign in front of it." Joanne Sandstrom, managing editor, Institute of East Asian Studies, University of California, Berkeley, reads her e-mail at work in Unix mail. She said, "E-mail messages beginning with 'From' have been garbled from time to time."

To test this bit of strangeness, I used Outlook Express on ATTBI to send the following message to two friends who use Outlook Express on Earthlink, one on a Mac and the other on a PC:

> Here's another e-mail test.
> From where I sit, this looks fine. How does it look to
>   you?
> Does the "From" have an angle bracket in front of it?

The message showed up on their screens like this:

> Here's another e-mail test.
> >From where I sit, this looks fine. How does it look
>   to you?
> Does the "From" have an angle bracket in front of it?

Although the ">From" anomaly seems to be fairly wide spread, it appears mysteriously, with no predictable pattern. Mark Levinson said, "I'm fairly certain that the '>' is inserted to prevent disruption from mail systems that interpret any line starting with 'From' as the beginning of a new message header." To avoid confusion, don't start lines or paragraphs with the word "From".

Attachments. Of course you and I always get permission from recipients before sending attachments, right? Or, if we know and correspond regularly with the intended recipients, we at least alert them that an attachment is on its way. But not all e-mail users are that conscientious. And not all e-mail servers, programs, and networks handle received attachments in the same way. As a result, unless certain precautions are taken, your business mail can be slowed down or lost.

Rhana Pike, publications officer, NHMRC Clinical Trials Centre, University of Sydney, Australia, said, "When I get e-mail messages that contain short, trivial, throw-away notes – and similar subject lines – I promptly delete them. Later on I sometimes discover that had I scrolled down, I would have found an attachment icon for something important. I think that if the icon is hidden at the bottom of the message, the writer should refer to the attachment in the subject line and early in the message, so that the reader knows to look for it."

A related problem was reported by Brenda Mercer, a business development specialist in the Washington, D.C. offices of an international accounting firm that uses the Outlook program. She said, "Recently, we received an e-mail with an attachment placed at the top, followed by the message. Other attached files were placed far below, under the auto-sig and with a good bit of blank space in between. We scrambled around for several days thinking that we did not have these files, because there was nothing immediately apparent to indicate a need to scroll down in the e-mail."

Ordinarily, when I receive attachments in Outlook Express, I know they are there because they're listed in an Attach field that appears directly under the Subject field, and because I have my message list options set to show a paper clip next to any message that contains an attachment. But in order to see the actual files attached, I must open them deliberately by clicking on their titles in the Attach field. On two isolated occasions, however, the attached material appeared in the message window itself, but below the signature. How did I know? When I reached the signature, the vertical scroll bar indicated that I had only viewed about one-tenth of the message. Sure enough, when I scrolled down, there – to my great surprise – were the complete attached graphics and text files.

Clearly, even if you are familiar with the usual procedures of recipients' e-mail programs, you can't be sure they will always act as expected. But you can avoid problems by indicating in the subject line and again in the beginning of the message that attachments are present. A subject line might say: Preliminary conference schedule - - 2 files attached; a first line might say: Two files attached.

By taking the precautions described in this chapter, you will gain some control over how your e-mail will look to recipients, and you will improve the chances that your messages will make sense when they arrive at their destination.

Formatting so they get what you send

- Set your options to use Plain Text, not HTML.
- Choose MIME encoding, not BinHex or UUencode.
- Set lines to wrap automatically at 65 to 75 characters.
- Choose a common, easy-to-read font set in regular style and at 11 or 12 points.
- Don't use colors (except the blue that automatically appears in links).
- Don't use symbols, bullets, tabs, tables, indents, italics, or bold.
- Use decimals instead of fractions, especially for mixed numbers.
- For italics, use underscores before and after the stressed word or phrase.
- For bold, use asterisks before and after the emphasized word or phrase.
- Write out all Internet addresses completely, including the http://, in the body of your messages and in your signature file.
- Don't begin lines or paragraphs with the word "From".
- If your e-mail includes attachments, in the subject line and again at the beginning of your message tell how many files are attached.

From *Business E-Mail: How to Make It Professional and Effective*
© 2002 by Lisa A. Smith

Making the e-mail parts work

Why devote a whole chapter to the parts of an e-mail message? You'd think figuring them out would be easy enough; but, judging from the responses to my survey of e-mail pet peeves, that is not the case. People manage to make errors of commission or omission in each of the parts and subparts – and thereby alienate recipients. In the corporate world, in your career, you can't afford to alienate others. Hence, this chapter.

To, CC, and BCC

The major mistake people make in these three fields is filling them too full. Don't be guilty of creating mailbox clutter. Perhaps your boss or all your subordinates don't really need to receive that CC (carbon copy) or BCC (blind carbon copy). A technical writer at a major aerospace company said, "The underlying issue here is common courtesy. Think about who has to see the message, who might like to see the message, etc. Don't include lots of folks as To, CC, or BCC recipients out of laziness. Take a few extra moments to really consider who should get the message."

Of course putting addresses in the CC field instead of in the BCC field may also be done out of courtesy; it allows the main recipient (in the To field) to know who else will receive the message. In fact, everyone who gets the message sees the e-mail addresses of all CC recipients. Just as with snail mail, you may want to send CCs for legal reasons or to ensure a wide paper trail.

You might also use the need-to-know doctrine advocated by government intelligence groups and the military when sharing sensitive or classified information: in work-related e-mail, tell people only what they must know to perform their jobs. When you originate a message directed within your company, ask yourself if everyone on your company list needs to receive it. Is the information proprietary? Perhaps the message pertains only to a particular department or team. The aerospace technical writer said, "It's easy to set up small mail groups. On one program I had a Demo group of about 10 people, a Systems group of about 15, a Training group of 5, and a Project group of 50 or so. No recipient sees all the other recipients' names, just the group name."

That's another advantage of using a group name instead of many individual names in the To field: each addressee doesn't have to scroll down past a long list of names, which may fill ten or more lines, to get to the message, which may be only two or three lines long.

When you answer a message that came through a company list, ask yourself if you really need to click on Reply All. Perhaps an individual reply would be just as effective and more appropriate. Rick Young, a director of print production at a large toy manufacturing company, said, "My pet e-mail peeve is the 'e-mail discussion.' A simple question to someone is forwarded to others who, in turn, forward it on, and the original question becomes a long thread that never seems to end. Each recipient replies to 'all' instead of just to 'sender,' thus ensuring that you will receive tons of e-mail about a simple question that by now has evolved into a topic that has no relevance at all."

For messages sent to people outside your company, the contents of the To field become even more important. Obviously, if your message contains proprietary information, you want to be sure that everyone in the To field is entitled to see it. You don't want to be guilty of revealing your company's trade secrets. And, of equal importance, if you are sending to a list that you generated yourself, and the people on the list do not know each other, you would be violating their privacy if you included their e-mail addresses in the To or CC field.

As Kathy Fitzgerald Sherman, author of *A Housekeeper Is Cheaper Than a Divorce: Why You CAN Afford to Hire Help and How to Get It,* said in a post to a publishers' list, "I was angered when I received a newsletter with the distribution list contained in the To field rather than in the BCC field. This is a serious violation of e-mail etiquette. It means that my e-mail address can now be harvested by each recipient of that newsletter! I wish everyone who sends mass e-mail would use the BCC field."

Not only could her e-mail address be used by anyone who received the newsletter, but they all now have information that is actually none of their business: the e-mail identities of all the subscribers. If you do any marketing via e-mail, through opt-in newsletters or any other message vehicle, take care that you don't inadvertently reveal the names or e-mail addresses of other clients or potential clients. People appreciate having their privacy protected.

You may generate a work-related e-mail list of people who don't work for your company but who know each other because they're all members of a particular committee or organization. Although you wouldn't be violating their privacy by showing all their names, you would be wasting space unless you placed the list in the BCC field.

Remember that different e-mail programs, ISPs, computers, networks, and various combinations of those factors may handle address lists and the BCC field in different ways. Ask your IT manager for help in setting up special lists, or do some testing on your own.

(Hint: You can try inserting your own address in the To field or creating and inserting a meaningful name that pertains to the list; then place recipients' addresses in the BCC field. If possible, avoid options that display "Undisclosed Recipient" in the To field; although that phrase is harmless, it may arouse suspicion in the minds of some of your addressees. For greatest efficiency, create a group name and load all the individual member addresses into that group. Then place the group name in the To field.)

The Subject Line

The major problem in the Subject field is just the opposite of the one in the To field. Too often, the subject line is not full enough. And on occasion, it's blank. An empty or vague subject line may be frustrating in personal e-mail. For corporate e-mail it can be devastating. At best, recipients may be annoyed. At worst, if the subject is not clearly identified, if it does not relate to the business at hand, if it does not pique the readers' interest, your message may not even be opened. As a result, your organization could lose business.

Remember that every e-mail you send to people outside of your company is a marketing message. The subject line plays a vital marketing role; its purpose is to make recipients want to open the mail and to give them an accurate preview of its contents. Since you wouldn't send business-related e-mail to strangers without their permission, you can safely assume that those on your To list have some interest in what your company offers. The more specifically your subject line relates to their interest (and, of course, to the content of your message), the more likely they are to open your e-mail. (Hint: Imagine that you have to send your whole message the old-fashioned way – by telegram. Each word will cost you $10, and you can't spend more than $80. What words will you choose to best convey your message? Use those words as your subject line.)

Inadequate subject lines can lead to other problems for recipients. Susan Squires, a developmental editor for a worldwide religious media organization, said, "Blank subject lines are high on my list of e-mail pet peeves. I save a lot of e-mail for future reference, and it's hard to refer to a message with no subject line. Subject lines that don't relate to the subject of the message are almost equally unhelpful for filing and retrieving."

In a similar vein, Rhana Pike, the publications officer at the University of Sydney NHMRC Clinical Trials Centre, said, "Flippant and uninformative subject lines, like 'another thought' or 'more of my stuff,' don't work. If my incoming e-mail isn't filterable, with a main heading and a subheading, it gets lost in the crowd or deleted as possible spam. Also, if I'm keeping a thread of messages about a particular project, the list of subjects should allow me to search for old messages easily. It's so time consuming to have to open each one when there are hundreds of them."

Subject lines like "an invitation," "a question," "an idea," or "misc" may be appropriate at times in personal messages to friends or family members, but in business e-mail – both within and outside of your company – you need to be more specific: "an invitation to our company picnic," "a question about the ABC project deadline," "an idea about reducing production costs," "misc. facts about the new widget." If you're sending a purchase order or invoice or any message that pertains to something numbered, include the number in the Subject field. Of course one thing you should not put in the subject line of an original message is the word "Re." Most e-mail programs insert "Re:" automatically when you click on "Reply"; the absence of "Re" lets the receiver knows that the message is the first one on a particular subject.

The subject line in replies presents additional problems that require your attention. Instead of automatically hitting the reply button, think about whether your response actually pertains to the subject named. When a message on a particular topic or thread goes back and forth several times or gets forwarded (with permission, of course) to several different people who join in the discussion, the subject often changes. Take the initiative to change the subject line so that it is pertinent again. To alert recipients to the fact that you have changed the name of an ongoing discussion, you can type the old subject line after the new one so that it looks like this:

Subject: Job #2374 (was Openings in production)

Ongoing threads often lead to absurd and meaningless subject lines, a phenomenon bemoaned by Fran Henry, a Colorado freelance writer and editor who supplied an example similar to the one below:

Fw: [Training] Re: [Training] Re: [Training] Re: [Training]
Fw: [Training] Purpose of October seminar?

Each time a member of that e-mail discussion group [Training] forwarded or replied to the message, the subject line expanded unnecessarily but automatically. If you find comparable subject lines on e-mail you receive, delete all the excess words before sending the messages on. (In those cases, you shouldn't include the old subject in parentheses.)

The Salutation

Is a salutation necessary in business e-mail? The answer is: It depends. If you're writing to someone within your company, then it depends on how often you correspond with that person and on where he or she stands within the company hierarchy in relation to you. It also depends on the corporate culture.

In most companies, you wouldn't need to use a salutation in messages to colleagues, subordinates, and others you deal with frequently. In most situations, it would be silly to begin an e-mail to your co-worker Kathy Brown, whose office is just down the hall from yours, with "Dear Kathy," although you might open with a friendly "K." On the other hand, if she were your immediate boss, you might spell out her name: "Kathy." Or, if she were higher on the corporate ladder and not someone you dealt with regularly, you might start with a formal greeting: "Dear Ms. Brown."

A good rule of thumb is to use the same level of formality in your salutation as you would in a face-to-face greeting.

The salutation sets the tone of your correspondence. Mentioning the addressee's name adds a warm, personal touch. Even the most formal correspondence need not be cold and without feeling. People like to see their names in print. They like to feel that you are talking to them in particular. But that special touch will be lost if you spell their names incorrectly. Is it "Sara" or "Sarah"? If you're not sure, call and ask.

Many people resent it, however, when strangers address them by their first names. In sending e-mail to people you don't know, therefore, begin with a safe degree of formality. You certainly don't want to offend clients or customers by being too familiar. Like a formal letter on hardcopy, a formal letter sent via e-mail should begin:

Dear Ms. Brown:

Notice that the salutation in formal business letters ends with a colon, not a comma. Even when you are on a first name basis with the addressee, you should still end the salutation of a business letter with a colon:

Dear Kathy:

When you've reached the point when less formality is needed, you might write:

Good morning, Kathy.

or even more informally:

Hi, Kathy.

Each of those two greetings takes the form of direct address, and each is a complete sentence; that's why you need to type a comma after "Hi" and "Good morning," and a period after "Kathy."

In all of your business writing, no matter how casual, it pays to be correct. Remember, your professional image and your company's reputation are on the line. Not everyone will notice errors in style or punctuation or spelling. But those who do notice may wonder: If you and your company don't pay attention to those details, if you are careless with your business correspondence, perhaps you aren't careful enough with other things – things that would have a direct affect on them, details involving quality of service or product or safety. Given a choice, people generally prefer to do business with companies that demonstrate care in all aspects of a transaction.

No salutation is required when writing an impersonal hardcopy or e-mail message to a department. After the inside address in a hardcopy letter you would write something like "Attention: Accounts Receivable." In an e-mail message, the fact that it was directed to the accounts receivable department would be noted in the To or the Subject field.

When sending your first reply to e-mail messages from strangers, use the same level of formality in your salutation that they used in theirs. If they didn't include a salutation, you don't need to either. Also, when messages on the same subject fly back and forth fast and furiously, no salutation is necessary.

The Body
When writing the message section of business-related e-mail, you can follow many of the rules that apply to writing business hardcopy. Use active rather than passive voice (more on that in another chapter). Phrase your ideas in positive rather than negative terms; be upbeat. Focus on the recipient's interests and needs rather than on your company's or yours. If your message is a marketing pitch, emphasize benefits rather than features.

The nature of the electronic medium, however, calls for some special rules. Reading on screen is different from reading hardcopy. Most e-mail windows are set to a much smaller size than the usual 8½ by 11 letter paper. On a typical monitor, the vertical space available for the main section of an e-mail message is only about four inches. And remember that horizontal lines should be set for no more than 75 characters (see page 29), which makes them considerably shorter than the lines in a regular hardcopy letter.

Limit your e-mail message to one subject – the one you have carefully defined in the Subject field. Limit the length of your message to two or three carefully crafted paragraphs (with double spaces between them). Readers may resent receiving long messages that require them to scroll down and up several times in order to absorb the information contained in them. An exception would be if your message included a list of numbered questions; in that case each question would form a short, separate paragraph. If you cannot avoid a lengthy message, then use the Subject field to let recipients know what to expect:

> Subject: Causes of the recent upswing in production in
> Plant D [long]

Recipients may then choose to save the message and read it later, when they have more time, or print it out.

Include everything important in the body, because postscripts don't work well in e-mail. When people read hardcopy letters, they often read the signature and P.S. first. Not so in e-mail. Chances are that a postscript would never be seen. Most people will not scroll below the signature.

If you want recipients to answer a question or take a particular action, state the question or call to action in your last line, just above your signature. A question or suggestion buried within a paragraph may be overlooked or forgotten.

If you include a Web link in your message, be aware that URLs longer than 65 characters may be broken up by the time they reach their destination. If that happens, only the first line of the URL might remain a live link (blue), and the section that wraps to the next line would be black. When recipients click on that partial live link, they will most likely be informed that the page they are trying to access cannot be displayed. You can get around this problem by providing a shorter link (instead of the longer one or in addition to it) with instructions about how to get from there to the specific page you want recipients to see.

If your preferences are set to include the original message in replies, keep the body of your messages shorter by deleting everything but the pertinent parts of the original – the parts you are going to address in your reply. Then alternate sections of the original and your reply so that they flow smoothly.

If your preferences are not set to include the original message, then copy the parts you will respond to and paste them into your reply. Don't expect people to remember what they've written to you. Include enough of their original message to have your reply make sense. Of course if you use this copy-and-paste method, then you must set the original sections apart by enclosing them in <angle brackets> like that.

It's not necessary to include the original header information (date, names of sender and receiver, subject) or the sender's signature in your responses. If you use AOL, messages you receive from other e-mail programs may include a long section at the bottom titled "Headers" (not to be confused with headers that appear at the top of documents); it's certainly not necessary to include that "Headers" section in your replies.

The Closing

Whether a closing is necessary and what it should consist of depend on what, if any, salutation you used. The two parts should correspond with each other: no salutation, no closing; informal salutation, informal closing; formal salutation, formal closing. Rick Kamen, author of *Heirloom Stories from the Harnessmaker's Son*, coined a clever informal closing: "E-ya later." When I mentioned it in a personal e-mail to a friend, he replied with "E-ya later, cybergator." Clever, perhaps. Or just silly. But too informal for business use. More appropriate closings include "Best regards," "Regards," "Cheers," and "Best wishes." A formal e-mail message that addresses recipients by their last names should end formally with "Sincerely," or "Yours truly". (Closings are followed by a comma. Note that the second word in a closing begins with a lowercase letter, like the "t" in "truly".)

The Signature

In business correspondence sent in hardcopy, if the salutation includes only the addressee's first name, then the handwritten signature should include only the writer's first name. So if I wrote on paper to "Dear Tracy," I would sign just my first name, Lisa. Of course my full name, Lisa A. Smith, would appear in the typed signature, just as Tracy's full name would appear in the inside address section. That same letter sent via e-mail could include the equivalent of a signed first name above the formal signature.

Depending on company policy, and on the size and nature of your business, you may or may not need to include a signature file in your interoffice e-mail. If you do, it will no doubt be different from the one you use in mail to outsiders. Most e-mail programs allow you to create several signature files. You might want to have one for the work-related e-mail discussion groups you belong to, another for vendors and suppliers, and a different one for clients and customers.

In the signature files you create for outsiders, provide your full name, title, company name, the company's full URL, and your e-mail address; some recipients' programs may show your name but not your address in the "From" field. If you want recipients to be able to reach you by means other than e-mail, then list your phone and fax numbers, and complete street address. Your signature can also include a one-line description of the service your company provides. And, as mentioned earlier, you may want to add a line of humor or a quote related to your business.

Your e-mail signature file can be a powerful yet subtle form of marketing. The trick is to design a file that gives all the necessary and desirable information in no more than four to six lines, with each line containing no more than 65 to 75 characters (including spaces).

Combine what you've learned in this chapter with generous amounts of courtesy and a little common sense, and your e-mail will be well received both literally and figuratively.

(Copy this page and post it at your workstation for easy reference.)

Use the parts of your e-mail to create a pleasing whole

- Does everyone in the To field need to get this e-mail?

- Are the CCs necessary for business or legal purposes?

- Don't send proprietary information or trade secrets to outsiders.

- Will names in the To or CC fields violate privacy?

- Create group lists to use with BCCs when appropriate.

- In replying to messages from lists, do you need to click on "Reply All," or would an individual reply be just as effective?

- Fill in the Subject field of every original message.

- Do not use "Re" in the subject lines of original messages.

- Does your subject line relate specifically to the content?

- Word your subject lines to spark interest among customers and clients and encourage them to open your messages.

- Does the subject of your reply still fit the content, or should you write a new subject line?

- Use the same level of formality in your salutation as you would if you met the recipient face-to-face.

- Keep the body of your message short, with each line no longer than 75 characters.

- In replies, include only the pertinent parts of the original.

- Use a closing that matches your salutation.

- Include an appropriate signature.

From *Business E-Mail: How to Make It Professional and Effective*
© 2002 by Lisa A. Smith

Following the rules for business e-mail

While driving north to my local post office this morning, I came to a four-way stop at the same time as another car that was coming from the east. According to California driving rules, the car on the right has the right of way, so I let it go first. If you want to drive without incident, you follow the rules of the road. Those rules prevent chaos and confusion.

The rules of writing have a similar purpose: to prevent confusion and misunderstanding. Lack of clarity in writing can cause minor or even major losses of time and money. In certain industries it might even cause physical injury. If you follow the rules and conventions of writing, your messages will be clear. Readers will understand you. They will not stumble over your words; they will not have to pause to try to figure out what you mean; they will not be put off by your style or usage. They will glide along on the smooth flow of words and thoughts you give them. By following the rules of writing, you help your readers save time and money.

Change happens
Language changes continually. People use old words in new ways and coin words to describe new technologies and events. All the e-words we use now, for example, didn't exist just a few years ago. Eventually, the writing guidelines and grammar rules change too, so that they match usage. Although most changes in language occur gradually, some seem to happen overnight, spurred by television and the Internet. A catchy commercial that's written or spoken incorrectly – either deliberately or out of ignorance – can quickly spread incorrect usage. Take the slogan "Think different"; it will probably play havoc with all those adverbs that end in "ly." To be grammatically correct, the slogan should say "Think differently."

People vary in their willingness to accept change in grammar and word usage, newly coined words, and other aspects of oral and written language. People who are well read generally follow the rules (even though they may not be able to articulate them); and they notice when others break them. Mistakes in speech grate on their ears; mistakes in writing offend their eyes.

Changes in language become acceptable in casual speech much sooner than in formal speech or writing. When US presidents speak off the cuff, they may break the rules of grammar. But their formal speeches, written or polished by professionals, are grammatically correct – on paper, at least.

What does all this have to do with writing business e-mail? You want to make a positive impression on your clients, bosses, or co-workers who may be traditional in their use of language. Since you probably don't know how most recipients of your work-related e-mail feel about language use, the wise thing to do is to write carefully and correctly. To do that, follow the rules and guidelines found in this book and in the references listed on pages 129–130.

The perils of rule breaking

You must know the rules before you can break them successfully. The key word in that last sentence is *successfully*. When you successfully break the rules of writing, readers will not notice the breach. And that's the secret: successful rule breaking does not call attention to itself.

In business writing, you may want to call attention to your new products, the benefits of your services, your competitive edge, or your excellence in customer care. But you don't want people to notice the mechanics of your communications. You don't want readers to trip over the structure of your writing – your grammar, punctuation, word usage, and spelling.

That's why you need to know the rules and follow them, even in e-mail. Sure, e-mail feels less formal than other written communications. But business is business no matter what method of communication you use and no matter how friendly you and your clients may be. Business e-mail that conforms to established conventions of writing will allow readers to focus on the substance of your message without being distracted by its structure.

Recently I needed to have some information changed on a Web site. I sent an e-mail to the appropriate person and requested the changes. Nothing happened. A week later I sent another e-mail and asked for an answer. Here's what I received:

> There is one change that did not make it up and that is for product A276 the price change did not take, It will go up in the next upload. Defiantly by next Tuesday (8/14). The reason why it takes so long to do an upload right now is because of the amount of changes being made by every one changing their content, with so many changes being uploaded, sometimes it can take 24hours to copy the data base over to the Internet. We have scheduled days to do uploads, normally Tuesdays but right now we are at the mercy of our programers to copy the new over the old so that we can upload it. Once we have our new system in place for making changes, the changes will be instantaneous.

> Once again I do apologies for your wait.

The person who wrote that response was trying to apologize (not "apologies") for the delay (not "wait") and explain the situation that caused it. But his attempt was ineffective because he did not follow the rules of writing. Instead, he wrote a long, rambling message riddled with errors in sentence structure, punctuation, and spelling – and the kinds of mistakes that force readers to stop, go back, read again, and wonder what exactly is being said. It definitely (not "Defiantly") makes me wonder if I should take my business elsewhere – to a company that will value my time and not waste it with unnecessarily long, poorly written messages.

A friend sent an e-mail to his ISP complaining about poor service. Here's the response he received:

> We do thank you for your understanding and patients
> while we do process your request.

"Patients"? "while we do process"? This was probably an automated response sent to thousands of complaining customers. My friend switched to another ISP. He decided not to trust a communications company that communicates so poorly.

Everyone makes mistakes at times. Typos happen. But if you want people to think of you as a credible and reliable businessperson, you must not make glaring errors. Knowing the rules of writing and being able to use them confidently does pay off.

E-mail conventions

Certain writing conventions pertain specifically to e-mail, especially business e-mail. For example, don't SHOUT. Writing with all capital letters is the equivalent of shouting. It's not polite, and it's more difficult to read than a combination of capital and lowercase letters. Many people will not even open an e-mail if its subject line appears in all caps, because so much spam is sent that way.

When you want to emphasize a word or phrase, type asterisks on either side of it. Do *not* type in all uppercase letters. Another way to indicate emphasis in e-mail is to type _underlines_ on either side of a word or phrase; those underlines are the equivalent of italics in other printed communications.

Business e-mail to clients and others outside of your company needs to be written more formally than the instant messages you send to co-workers. In business e-mail, you need to follow the same conventions that you would in regular business letters. Capitalize the word "I" and all proper nouns (names of people, places, and organizations). Begin sentences with capital letters as a signal to readers that a new thought has begun. (I heard about an employee who tried to excuse his use of all lowercase in his e-mail messages to clients by saying he was too tired to press the shift key. As you can imagine, he didn't last long.) It's more difficult to read all lowercase letters than a combination of lower- and uppercase letters. Use appropriate punctuation to signal the end of the sentence (see Chapter 7). By following these rules, you make it easier for people to read your messages quickly.

Also, in formal business e-mail, spell words in the conventional way; save the shortcuts for instant messaging. You (not U) will maintain a mature, professional image by adhering to convention in your business writing.

Emoticons – those cute symbols, like smiley faces, that are formed by using combinations of punctuation marks – and initialisms like LOL or <grd> generally do not belong in business e-mail. Although some may have entered the general culture, many have not. If you don't know the people you're sending e-mail to, then you don't know if they understand or will appreciate the symbols and initialisms. For the sake of clarity, don't use them.

International mail
Take special precautions to prevent misunderstandings if your messages will be sent internationally. Spell out dates. In the United States, 5/7/02 means May 7, 2002; but in many other countries, including Britain, it means July 5, 2002. To avoid confusion or a sense of exclusion, do not include references to American culture or to local events that have not made world news unless those matters relate to your message. To ensure clarity, avoid slang, idioms, and regionalisms.

Prevent a red face
Finally, read your messages carefully before clicking the send button. Inadvertently sending incorrect or incomplete messages can be embarrassing; it can even get you into trouble. What if, for example, you mistakenly sent a message in which you typed a price as $195 instead of $295? In AOL, when you send a message to another AOL user, you can retrieve it if the recipient has not yet opened it; but other e-mail programs don't give you that second chance. Some programs offer other options. For example, in the PC version of Outlook Express, you can click on File | Work Offline to prevent a message from being sent accidentally while you're writing it.

What if no such option exists in your e-mail program? You can reduce the chance of errors in an important message or in one that will be sent to many people outside of your company by writing it as a text only (ASCII) file in your word processor first. Then spell check it, proofread it, and copy and paste it into your e-mail.

It's a good idea to proofread those important messages on hard copy as well as on screen. Read your message out loud if possible; whisper if you have to. And read it very slowly, pronouncing every syllable. That will help you catch typos and any words that you may have left out by mistake.

Fit the medium to the message

Even if you know that the person you're writing to generally prefers e-mail to other methods of communication, certain situations simply don't lend themselves to e-mail. A note of condolence, for example, should be handwritten. And everyone appreciates receiving a handwritten invitation or thank-you note. In fact, because they are so rare nowadays, handwritten notes tend to make an even more favorable impression than they used to. Which are you more likely to remember: an e-mail message, a computer-generated letter, or a handwritten note?

(Copy this page and post it at your workstation for easy reference.)

Rules for Writing Business E-mail

- Don't SHOUT. Use asterisks for *emphasis.*

- Begin sentences with capital letters.

- Begin proper nouns (names of particular people, places, organizations, or events) with capital letters.

- Capitalize the first person singular pronoun (I).

- End sentences with appropriate punctuation.

- Spell words in the conventional way; don't use shortcuts.

- Avoid cute symbols and initialisms (LOL).

- For international mail, spell out dates.

- Proofread messages for accuracy before clicking the send button.

- Be sure your message fits the medium.

From *Business E-Mail: How to Make It Professional and Effective* © 2002 by Lisa A. Smith

Part 2: How to write for business

Introduction

If you're one of those people who shudders at the word "grammar," listen up. Although using good grammar can not guarantee your professional success, poor grammar can prevent your career from taking off.

You probably know more about grammar than you think you do. And you may need to learn a little more if you want to be sure that your important business e-mail messages and other written communications make sense. Standard English has become the language of business throughout the world. Certainly you should use it – and use it correctly – in your business writing.

The four chapters that follow provide a selective guide to grammar. You'll find information about how to fix or avoid some of the most common problems found in business writing. To learn even more, check out the grammar books listed in the reference section of this book.

Think of grammar and syntax (word order within sentences) as the nails that hold the structure of your writing together. If your grammar and syntax are correct, the structure will be strong; if they're incorrect, the structure will be weak and wobbly. If you put your words in the wrong order, they won't say what you want them to say. If you use the wrong words, you may be misunderstood. If you punctuate incorrectly, your sentences may not make sense. And if your sentences don't make sense, you may mislead or lose clients. So stick with me here; you may even find that learning to write better will help you think more clearly. I know it will boost your self-confidence on the job.

Grammar: What the parts mean

You probably learned about the parts of speech and other grammatical terms in school, and most likely you've forgotten much of what you learned. To jog your memory and help you understand Chapters 6, 7, and 8, I'll define the parts of speech and the parts of sentences in this chapter, and give examples of how to use most of them. Some grammarians might argue with my definitions or find them incomplete or oversimplified, but you won't. You will find more than enough information in this section to help you write superb e-mail and other business communications.

Nouns: Nouns name people, places, and things. There are two kinds of nouns: common and proper. Common nouns name people, places, and things in general: boys, cities, chairs. Common nouns also name nonmaterial things like love, cooperation, ambition, and sincerity. Common nouns can be singular (child, desk) or plural (children, desks).

Proper nouns name particular people, places, and things: Michael, Philadelphia, Steelcase. Your name and the name of your company are proper nouns. The rule, established long before the advent of dot-coms, says that proper nouns should begin with a capital letter. Now some company names begin with a lowercase "e," which makes it awkward and potentially confusing to use the official form of those names at the beginning of sentences. Rewrite to avoid the problem.

> Wrong: eCompanyName showed good earnings for
>   the last quarter.
> Correct: For the last quarter eCompanyName
>   showed good earnings.

Pronouns: Pronouns take the place of nouns. There are three cases of pronouns: subjective (nominative), objective, and possessive. The function of a pronoun in a sentence (the way it's used) determines its case.

• Use subjective case pronouns as subjects: he, she, they, I, we, it, you, who, whoever.

> He ran for political office. (*He* is the subject of the
>   verb *ran*.)
> My vote goes to the person who works hardest. (In
>   this sentence, *who* is the subject of the verb
>   *works*.)

• Use objective case pronouns as the objects of verbs and of prepositions: him, her, them, me, us, you, whom, whomever.

> I drove him home. (Here, *him* is the object of the
> verb *drove*.)
> He works for them. (Here, *them* is the object of the
> preposition *for*.)

If you're not sure whether to use an objective or subjective case pronoun in a series of nouns and pronouns, try using the pronoun by itself.

> Wrong: John works for Brent, Sal, and I. (You
> wouldn't say John works for *I*.)
> Correct: John works for Brent, Sal, and me. (The
> objective case pronoun *me* is the object of the
> preposition *for*.)

To be grammatically correct – and polite – when referring to yourself and others, put yourself last:

> Wrong: The result was a tie between me and him.
> Correct: The result was a tie between him and me.
> (The objective case pronouns *him* and *me* are both
> objects of the preposition *between*.)

> Wrong: He gave me, Kate, and Tom a raise.
> Correct: He gave Kate, Tom, and me a raise. (*Kate,*
> *Tom,* and *me* are all objects of the verb *gave*.)

Again, if sentences like that last one give you trouble, try writing them without referring to others. You know you'd never say *He gave I a raise.*

Using *whom* and *whomever* can sound stilted in informal writing. And they're rarely used correctly in informal speech.

Correct: For whom do you work? (In this sentence,

whom is the object of the preposition *for*.)

Common usage: Who do you work for?

Who is technically wrong in that sentence because the subjective case shouldn't be used as the object of *for*, but it sounds less stuffy to the modern ear. So go ahead and break the rule in all but the most formal writing.

• Reflexive or intensive pronouns end in *self* or *selves* – myself, herself, himself, ourselves, themselves, itself – and they can cause problems.

Don't use reflexive pronouns as subjects.

Wrong: Susan and myself attended the sales

meeting.

Correct: Susan and I attended the sales meeting.

How can you tell if you've got it right? Say the sentence with just the pronoun, and see how it sounds. You'd certainly never say or write *Myself attended the sales meeting;* therefore don't say *Susan and myself attended.*

Don't use reflexive pronouns as the object of a verb.

Wrong: The group chose myself.

Correct: The group chose me.

Use reflexive pronouns to refer back to the subject of the sentence.

Correct: Paul drove himself to the station.

Correct: They drove themselves to the station.

Correct: She gave herself permission to be late.

Use reflexive (intensive) pronouns to intensify or add emphasis to what you say.

Correct: I myself believe his theory.

Correct: I want to do it myself.

Correct: He himself took charge.

And use reflexive pronouns as objects of prepositions when the pronouns reflect back to the subject.

Correct: He wrote the speech by himself.

Correct: She sent a BCC to herself.

• Possessive pronouns – hers, his, its, yours, theirs, mine, ours – can cause trouble because, unlike possessive nouns, they do not take apostrophes. In particular, note that the possessive pronoun *its*, which means *belonging to it*, does not have an apostrophe. (With an apostrophe, *it's* means *it is*.)

Correct: Its owner was a conglomerate.

Correct: The new law was weaker than its precursor

Correct: The large office was hers alone.

Correct: Is that briefcase yours?

Correct: Theirs is the larger office.

Use possessive pronouns in front of gerunds (*ing* words).

Wrong: I like the idea of him going to the moon.

Correct: I like the idea of his going to the moon.

Wrong: We supported them purchasing the equipment.

Correct: We supported their purchasing the equipment.

• Demonstrative pronouns – this, that, those, these – demonstrate or point to what you're talking about.

> This tie goes with that shirt.
> Those belts match these shoes.

• Relative pronouns – that, which, who, whom – are used to begin clauses that describe nouns or pronouns. Using the correct relative pronoun helps to avoid confusion. Use *that* to begin clauses that are necessary to describe the subject.

> In this sentence, the word that begins the clause is
> *that.*

Without the clause *that begins the clause,* that sentence wouldn't make much sense, would it? In other words, the clause describing *word* is necessary. Those necessary clauses are called *restrictive.* Restrictive clauses limit the subject of the sentence. Restrictive clauses may begin with *that* or *who.* Note that no punctuation separates restrictive clauses from the subjects they describe.

> The keyboard that works best for him is ergonomic.
> The boy who cried wolf was ignored.

That last example tells you that only one particular boy was ignored. The ignoring is restricted or limited to one boy. The descriptive clause *who cried wolf* is a necessary description of the subject *boy.*

➤ Note: Use the pronoun *who* to refer to people; use *that* for everything else.

> Wrong: The woman that ran for office works for my
> company.

Correct: The woman who ran for office works for my
company.

Wrong: The company who sponsors the team issued
a statement.

Correct: The company that sponsors the team
issued a statement.

Wrong: A bear who roller skated amused the crowd.
Correct: A bear that roller skated amused the crowd.

When descriptive clauses are not necessary, they are
called *nonrestrictive*. Nonrestrictive clauses give extra information about the subject, information that is not needed in
order to understand the sentence. Nonrestrictive clauses
may begin with *which* or *who*. They are set off by commas.

The boy, who wore a red shirt, was ignored.

The fact that the boy happened to wear a red shirt is
immaterial to his being ignored.

The direct mail campaign, which lasted a month,
brought in many new clients.

The nonrestrictive clause *which lasted a month* gives extra
information that the reader does not need in order to
understand the main thought of the sentence.

Not all writers, editors, or grammarians insist on the convention of using *that* to introduce restrictive clauses and
using *which* to introduce nonrestrictive clauses surrounded
by commas. But I do; I think it results in clearer writing, and
I'm in favor of any rule that leads to clarity. Also, you should

know that the convention is fairly new; you will not find it in much old writing – the Declaration of Independence, for example.

Verbs: Verbs express action: go, make, buy, act, spend, subscribe, order, merge, hire, communicate. They can also express a state of being, like the various forms of the verb to be: is, was, would have been, will be. Other verbs – feel, smell – can express either an action or a state of being.

> Bill felt exhilarated. (state of being)
> Bill felt the vibrations. (action)
> The baby smelled like talcum powder. (state of
>   being)
> The shopper smelled the cantaloupes. (action)

Infinitives are verbs with *to* in front of them – to go, to stay, to dream. Gerunds are verbs that end in the letters *ing* – working, sleeping, talking, driving; they serve as nouns.

> Working allowed Jim to improve his skills. (The
>   gerund *Working* serves as the noun subject in this
>   sentence.)
> The commotion outside prevented George from
>   sleeping. (The gerund *sleeping* serves as the noun
>   object of the preposition *from*.)

Verbs have voice. When the subject of the verb does the acting, then the verb is in the active voice. When the subject is acted upon, then the verb is in the passive voice. Passive voice combines a form of the verb *to be* with the past participle of another verb.

Active: She completed her presentation. (The
    subject, *She,* acted.)
Passive: Her presentation was completed. (The
    subject, *presentation,* was acted upon.)

Active: Laura taped her speech.
Passive: Laura's speech has been taped.

To create dynamic, compelling, powerful writing, use the active voice as much as possible. Passive voice is – well, it's passive; it sounds weaker and less decisive than active voice. Marketing communications generally rely heavily on active voice.

Adjectives: Adjectives modify (describe, set apart, limit) nouns and pronouns. Most often, adjectives – small, round, red, happy – come before the nouns they modify.
    The happy child danced through the sunny room.
        (The adjectives *happy* and *sunny* modify the
        nouns *child* and *room.*)

But adjectives also come *after* verbs that express states of being.
    Tom felt happy. (The adjective *happy* describes
        Tom's state of being.)
    Later he was sad. (The adjective *sad* describes his
        state of being.)
    Tom feels well. (Here *well* serves as an adjective that
        means *in good health,* and *feels* serves as a
        state-of-being verb.)

Adverbs: Adverbs modify verbs, adjectives, and other adverbs. Many – but not all – adverbs end in *ly*.

> The incredibly happy boy danced unbelievably lightly over the rocks. (The adverb *incredibly* modifies the adjective *happy*; the adverb *unbelievably* modifies *lightly*, which is also an adverb; *lightly* modifies the verb *danced*.)
>
> Andrew writes well. (In this sentence, *well* serves as an adverb that means *capably*; it modifies the action verb *writes*.)

Conjunctions: Conjunctions connect words, phrases, or clauses. Some common conjunctions are *and, but, or, so, yet, because, if, unless, since.*

> Printers and monitors were on sale. (The conjunction *and* connects two words.)
>
> Leave the papers on the desk or on the floor. (The conjunction *or* connects the two phrases beginning with *on.*)
>
> Do it because I said so. (The conjunction *because* connects the two clauses *Do it* and *I said so.*)

Prepositions: Prepositions describe how nouns or pronouns relate to each other or to other parts of a sentence. Some words commonly used as prepositions include *to, in, of, at, for, with, on, off, over, under.*

➤ Note that you may end a sentence with a preposition, particularly when it would sound stilted or awkward if you didn't. The story goes that when someone reminded Winston Churchill about the old rule to the contrary, he responded mockingly, "That is a rule up with which I will not put." I'm going to end this sentence with a preposition as further proof of whose side I'm on. You can do it too, when it sounds right.

Interjections: Interjections are those little words that stand by themselves and are most often followed by an exclamation mark: Oh! Brrrr! Ouch! Stop! Well! Don't! Interjections usually express strong emotion; expletives (swear words) are often interjections.

Articles: Articles are those little words — *the, a, an* — that appear in front of nouns. The first one, *the*, is a definite article; the other two are indefinite articles. Use *a* in front of words that start with the sound of a consonant (regardless of how they are spelled) — a shoe, a desk, a hero, a use, a European. Use *an* in front of words that start with the sound of a vowel — an issue, an academy, an overview, an eagle. The one exception is the word *historical*, which may be preceded by *an*. But even that exception is disappearing, so you really don't need to worry about it.

➤ Note that some words can be used as more than one part of speech depending on the role they play in particular sentences.

> His left hand was not as strong as his right. (Here, *left* is an adjective that modifies the noun *hand*.)
> The supervisor left the building. (Here, *left* is an action verb.)

Sentences: A sentence is a group of words that expresses a complete thought; it may be expressed as a statement, a question, or an exclamation.

> Jackie left the office early. (statement)
> Did Jackie leave the office early? (question)
> Jackie's gone! (exclamation)

A sentence contains a subject and predicate. The subject may be a noun, a pronoun, or a noun phrase. The predicate contains a verb. Of course both the subject and predicate may contain other words or groups of words.

Sentences may be simple, compound, or complex. A simple sentence contains just one subject and one predicate, and it may have as few as two words: a noun or pronoun as the subject and a verb as the predicate.

> Zoe smiled. (The subject is the noun *Zoe*; the
>   predicate is the verb *smiled*.)

A simple sentence can also have many more words.

> An ecstatic Zoe and her sister Anna smiled at the
>   thought of Duncan's homecoming. (The subject is
>   *An ecstatic Zoe and her sister Anna*; the predicate
>   is *smiled at the thought of Duncan's homecoming*.)

A sentence can have a compound subject in which the parts are usually connected by *and*.

> Zoe and Kate smiled. (*Zoe* and *Kate* make up the
>   compound subject.)
> Zoe, Kate, and Duncan were reunited. (The
>   compound subject here contains three elements:
>   *Zoe, Kate,* and *Duncan*.)

➤ Note that subjects and predicates should not be separated by commas.

Wrong: Zoe and her sister, were happy.

Correct: Zoe and her sister were happy.

A compound sentence contains two or more independent clauses. A clause is a group of words that contains a subject and predicate. An independent clause can stand alone as a sentence. The two (or more) independent clauses of a sentence may be connected by a conjunction (*and, but, or*) that is preceded by a comma.

Zoe smiled, but Duncan did not look pleased.

Duncan frowned, and Zoe looked worried.

➤ Note that because it is perfectly correct to begin a sentence with a conjunction, you could break those sentences into two shorter ones.

Zoe smiled. But Duncan did not look pleased.

Duncan frowned. And Zoe looked worried.

You may also connect independent clauses by a semicolon, with no conjunction.

Zoe smiled; Duncan did not look pleased.

Duncan frowned; Zoe looked worried.

Several independent clauses may be connected by commas alone if each clause is short and all are of the same simple structure.

He came, he saw, he conquered.

But be careful if you leave out the conjunction. You run the risk of creating a run-on sentence, also known as a comma splice, because most independent clauses cannot be connected by a comma alone. You usually need to use a conjunction – or a semicolon – between the clauses.

> Wrong: Steve took the elevator, Donna climbed the stairs. (This is a run-on sentence.)
> Correct: Steve took the elevator, and Donna climbed the stairs.

> Wrong: Marley played the piano, Tracy sang along.
> Correct: Marley played the piano; Tracy sang along.

If a sentence contains just two, short, independent clauses, you may connect them by a conjunction without a comma.

> She walked and he drove.
> She worked but he rested.
> Will you go or shall I?

A dependent clause cannot stand alone; it depends on the independent clause in the sentence to make sense. A complex sentence contains an independent and a dependent clause.

> While Sue drove, Frank studied the map. (The dependent clause *While Sue drove* cannot stand alone; it wouldn't make sense without the independent clause *Frank studied the map.*)
> Alice explained the procedure as she showed the slides. (Here the dependent clause comes at the end of the sentence.)

There are different kinds of dependent clauses; each may act as a different part of speech in the sentence.

Whoever loses pays the piper. (The dependent
clause *Whoever loses* is a noun clause and acts as
the subject of this sentence.)

The award goes to whoever gives the best speech.
(The dependent clause *whoever gives the best
speech* is also a noun clause; it acts as the object
of the preposition *to*.)

The papers that Jeff filed could not be found. (The
dependent, restrictive clause *that Jeff filed* acts as
an adjective modifying *papers*.)

The files, which had been alphabetized, contained
information about repeat clients. (The dependent,
nonrestrictive clause *which had been alphabetized*
also acts as an adjective; it modifies *files*.)

Jeff worked late because he wanted to find the
missing files. (The dependent clause *because he
wanted to find the missing files* acts as an adverb.)

When Jeff found the files, he placed them on Hank's
desk. (The dependent clause *When Jeff found the
files* also functions as an adverb.)

Sentence Fragments: Earlier I said that a sentence must
express a complete thought and must contain a subject and
predicate. Well, you may break that rule sparingly, but you
must have a good reason to do so. At times you may want to
use a sentence fragment – a partial sentence instead of a
whole one – to create drama or suspense or variety or
emphasis.

What a day! Sara was hired, fired, rehired, and given
a raise all within six hours. (*What a day* is an
acceptable sentence fragment in this context.)

How thoughtful of you to acknowledge my
   promotion! Thank you for the plant. It's perfect
   for my new desk. (This example also begins with
   an acceptable sentence fragment. The fragment is
   more graceful than the usual phrasing *It was
   thoughtful of you to acknowledge my promotion.*)
She found a job, an apartment, a roommate, and a
   new car in just one day. All thanks to Greg. (*All
   thanks to Greg* is the fragment here.)

That last fragment is not as strong as the one in the previous examples. *All thanks to Greg* could easily be handled in a more acceptable way: set off by a comma or by a dash, for emphasis.

Here's a good rule of thumb: No business communication should contain more than two sentence fragments.

Syntax: Putting the parts together

Now that you know the rules of the road, you can learn to operate the vehicle of language smoothly. Your clients, customers, and co-workers will then be able to navigate through all your business communications without being stalled, misled, or stopped.

Plurals

Remember what I said earlier about this being a selective guide? Well, I'm going to be especially selective in this section. Some plurals are irregular: wives, children, mice, oxen, teeth, feet. But most plurals, including the plurals of compound words, are formed by adding s or es: hairdos, books, classes, potatoes. Even dates, abbreviations, and acronyms are now made plural by adding just an s.

The company reorganized in the 1980s and hired
    three more CPAs in the 1990s.
Two UFOs were reportedly seen in the desert.
Joe explained the ABCs of the plan.
Kirby settled all his IOUs after winning the lottery.
Mix two teaspoonfuls of sugar in two cupfuls of
    milk.
The two mothers-in-law compared notes.

There is only one exception: When confusion might result, form the plural by adding 's. Therefore, when writing plurals of numbers, letters, and abbreviations with periods, you add an apostrophe before the s.

They bought size 10's and 20's.
Mind your p's and q's.
Three students received Ph.D.'s.

To repeat: Those apostrophes are added only to avoid confusion.

The plurals of ordinary words never take an apostrophe. I'll say it again: Do not use an apostrophe when writing the plural of an ordinary word. (Can you tell this is one of my pet peeves?)

Possessives

Now you can let loose with those apostrophes; in fact, with one exception that I'll explain later, you have to use apostrophes to form possessives. Form the possessive of singular common nouns by adding 's.

The sun's backlighting outlined the creature's shape.
The company's representatives lobbied for the bill's
    passage.

Form the possessive of most singular proper nouns in the same way.

Joel's hiring depended on Bruce's departure.

Mavis's office used Patty's services.

Particular proper nouns that end in the letter *s* take only an apostrophe, however, without the extra *s*: Jesus' word, Moses' followers. Other exceptions include words that you're not likely to use in your business communications.

To form the possessive of plural nouns, both common and proper, that end in *s*, add just an apostrophe.

The Joneses' business thrived in its new location.

The Murphys' building was older than the Davises' building.

The printers' salespeople met the publishers' representatives.

The ladies' purses matched their shoes' colors.

But to form the possessive of plural nouns that do not end in *s*, add *'s*: oxen's yokes, children's toys.

When possession is held jointly by two or more, add the indication of possession only to the last name or noun.

Are you going to the meeting in Sara and Dave's office?

Their industry magazine printed Cathy and Doug's article.

The cat and dog's owner kept both animals inside.

Now here is the exception to the rule about possessives and apostrophes: Possessive pronouns – its, hers, yours, theirs, ours – do not take apostrophes.

The dog searched for its bone.
Is the fault theirs or ours?
The problem is neither hers nor yours.

Parallelism

One of the most frequent grammatical goofs found in written business and marketing communications is lack of parallelism. In writing, parallelism means that all elements in a series need to be grammatically or structurally the same. All items in a series should be the same part of speech or be phrased in the same way.

Wrong: He likes to ski, biking, to swim, and a hike.
Correct: He likes skiing, biking, swimming, and hiking.

Parallelism also means that all the elements in a series should be part of the same thought.

Wrong: On our Web site you can sign up for our newsletter, order products, enroll in a course, and it's easy to use. (What you can do on the site is one thought; the fact that the site is easy to use is a separate thought and, therefore, should not be part of the series.)
Correct: On our easy-to-use Web site, you can sign up for our newsletter, order products, and enroll in a course.

Parallelism applies to lists as well as to sentences. One item in the list that follows is not parallel in structure to the rest; therefore, that item needs to be rewritten. Can you tell which one it is?

1. Write a letter.
2. Copy the memo.
3. Going for a walk.
4. Plan the agenda.
5. Buy toner.

Agreement

Pronouns and antecedents. Pronouns should agree with their antecedents (the words they refer to) in number and gender. Take this sentence, for example:

Everyone wants to have their work recognized.

In that sentence the plural pronoun *their* refers to the singular antecedent *Everyone*. The sentence breaks the rule. Yet many people would be comfortable hearing or saying it that way in casual conversation.

This is a good example of language change in progress. The change was prompted by people's efforts to avoid using male pronouns when referring to both men and women. It may be politically correct, but it's not grammatically correct.

In business writing and other formal writing, therefore, it would be better to reword the sentence so that it didn't break any rules. It could say:

All employees want recognition for their work.

In that sentence the plural pronoun *their* refers to the antecedent *employees*, a noun that is also plural.

Changing singular antecedents like *everyone* and *each* to plural nouns like *people* and *co-workers* is one easy way to stick to the rules. Here are some examples of how you can reword sentences to correct this type of problem in formal business writing:

Wrong: Each worker should wear their name tags.
Correct: All workers should wear their name tags.

Wrong: Each is responsible for their own
        presentation.
Correct: Speakers are responsible for their own
        presentations.

Wrong: Everyone who plans to attend must send in
        their registration forms by Friday.
Correct: If you plan to attend, please send in your
        registration form by Friday.

Wrong: Anyone who postmarks their order by
        Friday will receive a 5 percent discount.
Correct: All customers who postmark their orders by
        Friday will receive a 5 percent discount.

Wrong: Somebody who writes owns the copyright
        without registering their material.
Correct: Writers own the copyright to their material
        even without registering it.

Of course if the sentence refers to just women or just men, then there is no need to use the plural pronoun *their*. For example:

Each woman serves as a mentor to her younger
        female colleagues.
Every man must bring his own towel to the gym.

And in some cases, you may want to use both the male and female pronouns to refer to a singular noun:

> Will the person who uses this workstation on
> Saturdays please leave his or her name and
> phone number at the front desk.

Subjects and verbs. Singular subjects go with singular verbs; plural subjects need plural verbs.

> Wrong: One officer run the meeting.
> Correct: One officer runs the meeting.
>
> Wrong: Both managers has large offices.
> Correct: Both managers have large offices.

In the previous examples – and in most sentences – the subject precedes the verb. In certain cases, however, the subject follows the verb. Then you must be particularly careful that subject and verb agree in number.

> Wrong: There's many people who want that
> position.
> Correct: There are many people who want that
> position.
>
> Wrong: There's two sides to every story.
> Correct: There are two sides to every story.

There's is the contraction of *There is* (and of *There has*). Just as you wouldn't say *There is two sides*, you should not use the contraction *there's* (meaning *there is*) when the subject refers to more than one person, place, or thing.

Sometimes, though, it's not that simple to decide if a verb should be singular or plural. Collective nouns – words such as company, crew, family, group, majority, number, and team – can be used with singular or plural verbs depending on whether you're talking about the collective as a whole or about the people or things within it as individuals.

Wrong: The company have a Web site.

Correct: The company has a Web site. (The site represents the company as a whole.)

Wrong: The development team was unable to agree on a plan.

Correct: The development team were unable to agree on a plan. (The individual members of the team were unable to agree with each other.)

You also have to be careful when the subject contains phrases modifying the noun; don't confuse the actual subject with the words that separate it from the verb.

Wrong: Each of the candidates were asked to speak. (The subject *Each* is singular. The plural *candidates* is not the subject; it is the object of the preposition *of*.)

Correct: Each of the candidates was asked to speak.

Wrong: A group of benefit plans were developed by the human resources department.

Correct: A group of benefit plans was developed. (The subject is *group*, which is singular, not *plans*, which is plural.)

The choice of singular or plural verb can determine the meaning of some sentences. For example, if two things were considered, you might write:

Asking for a raise and flextime were considered. (The
compound subject, consisting of *Asking for a raise*
and *flextime,* takes the plural verb *were.*)

If two things were asked for, however, you would write:
Asking for a raise and flextime was considered. (The
subject is Asking, not raise and flextime, and
Asking is singular.)

In certain situations – in an *either . . . or* construction, for
example – you can let the subject closest to the verb determine whether it should be singular or plural. This is called
proximity agreement.
Either the vice president or the managers have to
attend. (The verb *have* agrees with the plural
subject *managers,* which is closest to it.)
Either the managers or the vice president has to
attend. (The verb *has* agrees with the singular
subject *vice president,* which is closest to it.)

And at times the plural sense of a singular noun – variety,
for example – combines with the plural noun closest to the
verb to determine that the verb be plural.
A variety of subjects were discussed during the
seminar.

But because *variety* is a singular noun, it would also be
correct to write:
A variety of subjects was discussed during the
seminar.

In other words, let common sense and your ear guide you in
choosing which verb to use.

Singular subjects take singular verbs even when modified by phrases that seem to make the subject plural.

> The department head, along with her assistant, was asked to resign. (The subject *department head* is singular; the phrase *along with her assistant* modifies the subject but does not make it a compound. Therefore the verb must be the singular *was*.)
> The division, including its six branches, was ready.
> The president, as well as her aides, is unavailable.

Compound subjects (subjects with more than one noun, pronoun, or noun phrase) take plural verbs.

> Walking and talking are her favorite activities. (The compound subject *Walking and talking* needs the plural verb *are*.)
> What she wants and what he needs are two different matters. (The two noun phrases *What she wants* and *what he needs* take the plural verb *are*.)
> He and she were both there. (The two pronouns *He* and *she* form a compound subject that needs the plural verb *were*.)

But there is an exception to that rule: If the word *each* or *every* precedes a compound subject, then it takes a singular verb.

> Each manager and supervisor has to write a report.
> Every rep and his aide has to attend the meeting.

Managing Modifiers

Modifiers are adjectives, adverbs, clauses, or phrases that describe, qualify, limit, or refer to other words. In business writing, an all-too-common mistake is the modifier that dangles. Here are four examples of dangling modifiers:

As a valued customer, we want to reward you with
    two months of free service. ("We" are not the
    valued customer; "you" are.)

Walking across the bridge, the ship could not be
    seen through the fog. (Since when can ships
    walk?)

His co-worker was honored for exceptional work by
    the company president. (Why was the co-worker
    honored for work performed by the president?)

Weighing only 20 pounds, the zoo attendant fed
    the newborn animal with a bottle. (That's one
    skinny zoo worker.)

Although a dangling modifier may make readers laugh, it's not so funny when the joke's on you or your company. Avoid the problem by placing modifiers next to the word or phrase they modify.

As a valued customer, you will receive a reward. We
    are going to give you two months of free service.
    (The modifier *As a valued customer* describes *you*.)

Walking along the shore, we could not see the ship
    through the fog. (The participial phrase *Walking
    along the shore* refers to *we*; the participle doesn't
    dangle when it's next to the word it describes.)

His co-worker's exceptional work was honored by
    the company president.

>   Weighing only 20 pounds, the newborn animal was
>   bottle fed by a zoo attendant. (It's the animal
>   that weighs only 20 pounds.)

Misplacement of modifiers leads to misunderstanding and confusion. The best place for modifiers is next to the word or phrase they modify. To avoid ambiguity, be particularly careful with the placement of the adverb *only*.

>   She only wore red on Thursdays.
>   She wore only red on Thursdays.
>   She wore red only on Thursdays.
>   She wore red on Thursdays only.

Which of those sentences says most clearly that she did not wear red on any other day of the week except Thursdays?

>   He only attends staff meetings on Mondays.
>   He attends only staff meetings on Mondays.
>   He attends staff meetings only on Mondays.
>   He attends staff meetings on Mondays only.

Which of those sentences say most clearly that he does not attend other kinds of meetings on Mondays?

To knowingly split an infinitive is fine. I just did it in that sentence: I put the adverb *knowingly* between *to* and the verb *split*. Careful writers split infinitives when the best place for the adverb is right in front of the verb it modifies.

>   To adopt effective production techniques easily was
>   the team's goal. (The adverb *easily* is too far from
>   the verb it modifies; splitting the infinitive by
>   saying *to easily adopt* would make the sentence
>   clearer.)

The applicant was able to listen and accurately
  respond to the questions. (The adverb *accurately*
  applies only to *respond* and not to *listen;* therefore
  it fits best in front of *respond* rather than after it.)

Careful writers do not split infinitives when there is no reason to do so, when the meaning remains the same without the split as with it, and when the split sounds odd or awkward.

Careless split: He tends to excessively worry.
Careful writing: He tends to worry excessively

If you put the parts of your sentences together carefully, if you write deliberately and knowingly, if you make your words say what you mean, then your business writing will be clear and easily understood.

Punctuation: Sending signals

Punctuation sends signals to your readers. When you want them to slow down or pause, you might use a comma or semicolon; when you want them to stop, you might use a period or a question mark or an exclamation point. To communicate clearly, without confusion, you must send the correct signals. That's why you need to know which signal to use when. What follows is a selected, alphabetical guide to punctuation that you will find useful for business writing. Note that I have not included the apostrophe here because its use and misuse with plurals and possessives was discussed in Chapter 6. And I don't include the ellipsis dots, used to indicate an omission in a quotation, because they're rarely needed in business writing.

[ ] Brackets
• Use brackets to enclose unquoted material in a quotation.

> According to the affidavit, "The CEO assured employees [in a memo dated 1/21] that there would be no layoffs in the first quarter."
>
> In her proposal, the human resources manager wrote: "These [three reasons for increased training requirements] include higher initial salaries, shorter probation periods, and lower educational requirements."

• Use brackets to enclose parenthetical comments within parentheses.

> (Remember that subjects and verbs must agree in number [see Chapter 6].)
>
> (Note that the equipment must warm up for 30 minutes before use [see page 39 in the user's manual].)

: Colon
• Formal salutations in business letters, including e-mail, end with a colon.

> Dear Mr. Patterson:
>
> Dear Judge Solomon:

• When the first part of a sentence introduces a thought that is explained in the second part, separate the parts with a colon, and start the second part with a lower-case letter.

> His speech was influential: listeners voted for him.
>
> Only one thing mattered: the outcome of the race.

• Introduce numbered or bulleted lists with a colon. Also use the colon to introduce lists within sentences.

> Management enforced three rules: no pets in the
> workplace on Mondays; no parking on the grass;
> and no online shopping during business hours.

When the items in the list are complete sentences, begin them with capital letters.

> Applicants were asked the following questions: Why
> do you want to work here? What special skills or
> experience do you have that fit the position to be
> filled? How much do you hope to earn five years
> from now?

➤ Note: The colon goes outside parentheses and outside quotation marks.

> Barbara understood the objective of the contenders
>   (all recent graduates): to secure high-paying
>   positions.
> Jeffrey found three unfamiliar words in the article
>   "Untouched by Fire": gnomon, kestrel, and scute.

, Comma

Misuse of the comma is rampant. Problems arise partly because comma usage can differ depending on whether you prefer an open style of punctuation or a closed style. Although I generally prefer the open style, which calls for less rather than more use of the comma, I also think that clarity must take precedence over style. Sometimes the comma appears when it shouldn't; sometimes it doesn't appear when it should. Let's start with the don'ts.

• Don't use a comma after a salutation in formal business correspondence.

>Wrong: Dear President Washington,
>Correct: Dear President Washington:

• Don't use a comma to separate subject and verb.

>Wrong: What he wants, is to succeed.
>Correct: What he wants is to succeed.

>Wrong: The reds, the blues, and the greens, all ran together.
>Correct: The reds, the blues, and the greens all ran together.

• Don't use a comma to separate two independent clauses unless the second clause is preceded by a conjunction (see Chapter 7 for more information).

>Wrong: Mark sent notices to all the committee members, Rhonda decided not to.
>Correct: Mark sent notices to all the committee members, but Rhonda decided not to.

• Don't use a comma around restrictive phrases.

>Wrong: The opening, posted yesterday, was filled immediately.
>Correct: The opening posted yesterday was filled immediately. (Yesterday's post [but no other posts] is the only opening being considered in this sentence; that's why the phrase is restrictive: it is needed in the sentence.)

• Don't set off names by commas when they are being used in a restrictive sense. For example, if you have two or more assistants (or friends or siblings), and you are writing about just one of them, there should not be a comma before and after his name.

> Wrong: My assistant, Fred, prepared the charts.
> (This says that you have only one assistant, and his name is Fred.)
> Correct: My assistant Fred prepared the charts. (This tells the reader that you have more than one assistant, but only Fred prepared the charts.)

➤ Note: When writing about your spouse or special partner, set his or her name off by commas; otherwise it will appear as if you have more than one.

> Wrong: Zoe's husband Eric joined the gym with her.
> Correct: Zoe's husband, Eric, joined the gym with her.
> Correct: Zoe's husband, Eric, and her friend Brian joined the gym with her. (Zoe has only one husband, but she has more than one friend, so *Brian* is not restrictive.)

• Use commas to set off nonrestrictive phrases (phrases that are not needed) but not restrictive phrases.

> Nonrestrictive: Prospective clients, who attended the free seminar, were given a tour of the facility.
> Restrictive: Prospective clients who attended the free seminar were given a tour of the facility.

The presence or absence of commas in the two preceding sentences affects their meaning. In the nonrestrictive sentence, *who attended the free seminar* is simply additional – but not necessary – information. In the restrictive sentence, the phrase is needed: the sentence says that the tour was restricted to those who attended the seminar.

• Use commas to separate items in a series. The classic – no doubt fictitious – example of the confusion that can result from omitting the serial comma is the book dedication "To my parents, Ayn Rand and God." For the sake of clarity, place a comma in front of the *and* or *or* that precedes the last item. To save space, newspapers do not use the serial comma in front of the last item, but you should. The final comma prevents the kind of misunderstanding and ambiguity found in the following examples.

> To fill the position of president, the search committee interviewed the rival's CEO, a micromanager and a friend of the committee's chairman.
> The university press considered publishing articles by a local physicist, a genius and a charlatan.

Was the rival's CEO both a micromanager and the chairman's friend? Or did the committee interview three people? Was the local physicist both a genius and a charlatan? Or was the press considering articles by three different authors?

When commas separate all items in a series – including the last one – confusion is avoided, as in the following:

> She dedicated her book to her parents, Ayn Rand, and God.
> The search committee interviewed the rival's CEO, a micromanager, and a friend of the chairman.

The university press considered articles by a local
physicist, a genius, and a charlatan.

Josh ordered pens, pencils, paper clips, and scratch
pads.

Sally saved the file to a disk, converted it to a PDF,
and sent it to Josh.

He wasn't sure whether to save it, copy and paste
it, or erase it.

• When two or more adjectives modify a noun in the same
way, separate them by commas. In other words, if it would
make sense to insert *and* between the adjectives, then insert
a comma.

The large, round, purple onion hung from a string.

In that example, each adjective [*large, round, purple*] has the
same relationship to *onion*. If the adjectives were separated
by *and*, the sentence would still make sense. But sometimes
what seems like an adjective is actually part of the element
being modified and should not be preceded by a comma.

Alicia was an intelligent, industrious working
woman.

In that sentence, the element being modified is *working
woman;* therefore no comma separates *industrious* and
working.

• Use a comma to separate independent clauses that are
connected by a conjunction.

Joe prepared the conference room, and William
ordered a catered lunch for the entire group.

• Use a comma after introductory clauses and phrases.

> Because he was leaving for a vacation on Saturday
>   morning, Bill worked late on Friday night to finish
>   the project.
> To complete the long project, Bill had to perform one
>   more test.
> By the end of the day, the goal had been reached.
> In 2005, 3005 will be hard to imagine.

• Use a comma to separate quoted speech from indirect speech. Note that the comma precedes the opening quotation marks but goes inside the closing quotation marks.

> When Jerry said, "Send in the clowns," everyone
>   laughed.

• Salutations in informal correspondence – and closings in all correspondence – are followed by commas.

> Dear Daddy,
> Sincerely,

➤ Remember: The comma separates elements, sets off nonrestrictive words and phrases, and signals readers to pause.

– — Dash

This is an em dash: —
This is an en dash: –
This is a hyphen: -

The hyphen is not a dash; I included it above just to show you how the three marks differ in size.

• Use em dashes to set off important words or phrases that interrupt the flow of a sentence. Unlike commas and parentheses, em dashes add drama by calling attention to the interruption. Note that there is no space between the em dash and the word that precedes or follows it. (To make an em dash in Word for Windows, hold down the Alt key and press 0151 on the number pad. In Word for the Mac, hold down the shift and option keys and press the hyphen.)

> I was writing a progress report one morning—it was during our busiest season—when Roger phoned with the good news.
> Traffic delays, crowded buses, disgruntled passengers—all that and more resulted from a strike by rapid transit workers.

• Use en dashes in the same way. But note that there is a space between the en dash and the word that precedes or follows it. I prefer using en dashes surrounded by spaces rather than em dashes because the en looks more graceful; I think em dashes look clunky, and they are too big to surround with spaces. (To make an en dash in Word for Windows, hold down the Alt key and press 0150 on the number pad. In Word for the Mac, hold down just the option key and press the hyphen.)

> Within the past three months, I've encountered several people – all women – with the same problem.
> I ventured to put some personal objects in my office – a major display of confidence.

➤ Note: Overuse of dashes lessens their dramatic effect. And of course in e-mail you should use hyphens, not dashes.

• Use the en dash, not the hyphen, to separate dates or geographical locations when you don't need to say the word *to* as you read the dash (see page 120).

> The 2001–2002 upswing in sales was remarkable.
>
> In fiscal year 2002–2003, the company switched to the accrual method of accounting.
>
> To get to the convention, Judith flew the San Francisco–Los Angeles–Mexico City route.

➤ Note: En dashes that separate dates or places should not be surrounded by spaces.

! Exclamation Point

Exclamation points indicate emphasis. Their use should be limited in any form of writing other than quoted speech. ("Hey! Watch out!" he shouted.) Use them sparingly in business writing. Whenever possible, let your words rather than your punctuation do the exclaiming. Exclamation points make writers sound breathless, and breathlessness does not sound professional. Never – never, never – use more than one exclamation point at the end of any sentence in business communication.

> Wrong: We're on schedule!!!
>
> Correct: We're on schedule!

- Hyphen

To follow the trend in American English (as opposed to British English), eliminate hyphens whenever possible in words with prefixes. Most *non* words, for example, can be correctly written without hyphens. In general, words with prefixes can be closed – written as one word without a hyphen – unless misunderstanding might arise. When in doubt, consult a dictionary.

Wrong: Eileen met her coworkers in the lobby.
Correct: Eileen met her co-workers in the lobby.

Wrong: Jared works for a publisher of non-fiction.
Correct: Jared works for a publisher of nonfiction.

Correct: They advertised their midsummer sale.
Correct: They held a sale in mid-August. (The
hyphen is needed because *August* begins with a
capital letter.)

• Use a hyphen to connect two words that form a phrase
used as an adjective, but don't connect those words when
they are not used as an adjective phrase.

Henry created the company's new credit-card
application. (The hyphenated adjective phrase
credit-card modifies *application*.)
Jeanne paid for the office supplies with a credit card.
High-school teachers have fun with their students.
(If *high-school teachers* were written without the
hyphen, you might think the teachers were high.)
Jack sold books to the local high school.
Jeremy was a small-business advocate. (If there were
no hyphen in *small-business*, readers might think
Jeremy was only five feet tall.)

• Do not use a hyphen when the first word in an adjectival
phrase is an adverb that ends in *ly*.

Wrong: Their goal was a fully-executed contract.
Correct: Their goal was a fully executed contract.
(The first word in the adjectival phrase *fully
executed* is the adverb *fully*.)

• Hyphens are used in certain compound words – two or more words used together to form one idea: sister-in-law, self-esteem, merry-go-round. Other compound words have become permanently bonded: middleman, paperboard, keyboard. Not all *middle, paper,* and *key* words have become solid compounds, however, just as not all *self* words are hyphenated. When in doubt, check it out – in the dictionary.

( ) Parentheses

• Use parentheses to enclose incidental information such as an aside, an example, or a short explanation. Commas and dashes can serve the same purpose; use your own judgment to decide which punctuation fits best in a given sentence.

> My partner's vacation (to the Bahamas) will not interfere with the production schedule.
>
> Various employee benefits (e.g., onsite childcare, exercise facilities, and parking; paid time off for volunteering; merchandise discounts) were being renegotiated.
>
> Expenses (see page 9 of the enclosed treasurer's report for a full list) did not exceed our expectations.

• Do not use any punctuation before the opening parenthesis except when the parentheses enclose numbers or letters in a series.

> Savings were noted in (1) daily expenses, (2) materials consumed, and (3) overtime outlays.
>
> Products were variously sorted by (a) color, size, and weight; (b) shape, material, and cost; and (c) country of origin.

• Parentheses can also be used to enclose whole sentences.
Expenses exceeded expectations by a considerable
amount. (For complete budget information, see
the enclosed report.)

. Period

In addition to its obvious use at the end of sentences, the
period is also used in abbreviations. That use, however, is
slowly declining. Academic degrees, for example, may now
be written without periods (PhD, MA, BA). In the US (or
U.S.), state abbreviations no longer require periods.

➤ Note: When an abbreviation with periods comes at the
end of a sentence, write only one period.

After many years of study he finally received his
Ph.D.
The game started at 4 p.m.

? Question Mark

In addition to its obvious use at the end of questions, you
may also use the question mark, enclosed in brackets, to
indicate that you question the correctness of what has just
been written.

The meeting was scheduled for Friday, October 9, [?]
at 2 p.m. (If your calendar shows October 9 as
Thursday instead of Friday, you would question
the accuracy of the statement.)

" " Quotation Marks

In addition to their obvious use to set off quoted speech and other material, quotation marks also set off (1) song titles, (2) titles of articles that are not published independently of books or magazines, (3) words that are used as words or in other special ways, and (4) the first appearance of made-up words.

> They sang their school song, "Arlington Reigns," at
>   the class reunion.
> His article, "Birds in the Bush," appeared in *National
>   Geographic*.
> She wrote the word "sunset" in the sand.
> John was acting like a "barlac" – a gross, impolite
>   fool.

➤ Note: In American English, periods and commas go inside the quotation marks except when the quoted word is cited as a word; then they go outside. Colons and semicolons go outside. Exclamation marks and question marks go outside unless they are part of the quotation.

; Semicolon

Semicolons are more forceful than commas; they give more importance to a break in a sentence than that given by commas.

• Use the semicolon to connect two independent clauses when the clauses are not connected by a conjunction.

> Jennifer set the agenda herself; she did not want our
>   suggestions.
> The diagnosis was largely one of elimination; there
>   was no test.

• Use the semicolon to separate items in a series when there are commas within the items themselves.

> The team colors were: Tigers, blue; Lions, red; Bears,
> green; Coyotes, brown.

/ Slash

Also called "solidus" and "virgule," the slash is another punctuation mark that should be used sparingly if at all in business writing. It may be used correctly to indicate a fraction ($^7/_8$) and to separate the parts of a date (12/20/06) in informal communications. But in formal business messages, careful writers will find other ways to say such things as "and/or" and "employer/employee relations."

> Poor: John and/or Jason will make the call.
> Better: Either John or Jason or both will make the
> call.

> Poor: There was a break in employer/employee
> relations.
> Better: There was a break in relations between
> employers and employees.

Word usage

Business writing in general, and e-mail messages in particular, should be short, simple, direct, clear, and easy to understand. The challenge is to say what needs to be said in as few words as possible. Make each word count. Use words that say exactly what you mean. To help you do that, in this chapter I will first present a few rules about word usage that apply particularly to business writing. Then I will give you examples of common phrases written in vague and passive language, and show how they can be rewritten using active and specific phrases. Next I will list commonly misused words and show how to use them correctly. And finally, I will list commonly confused words and explain when to use each one.

Six Rules about Words

1. Be specific. Omit vague, meaningless words such as *very* and *really*.

2. Keep it simple. Used correctly, short, simple words are powerful. For example, when you mean *use*, say *use*, not *utilize*. *Use* and *utilize* are not synonymous. Consult a good dictionary to learn the difference.

3. Don't be wordy; omit unnecessary words. Avoid *It is* and *There are* whenever possible. Be concise.

    Wordy: It is Arnold's intention to run for office.
    Concise: Arnold intends to run for office.

    Wordy: At this point in time I think we should
       change the rules.
    Concise: Now I think we should change the rules.

    Wordy: This is the place where the meeting took
       place.
    Concise: The meeting took place here.

    Wordy: You will want to avoid sentences that start
       with *It*.
    Concise: Avoid sentences that start with *It*.

4. Don't be redundant.
    Redundant: Free gift
    Correct: Free
    Correct: Gift

Redundant: The meeting starts at 8:00 a.m. in the
    morning.
Correct: The meeting starts at 8:00 a.m.

Redundant: The reason why it will rain is that a low
    is approaching.
Redundant: The reason is because a low is
    approaching.
Correct: The reason it will rain is that a low is
    approaching.

Redundant: She is a person who prefers small
    gatherings.
Correct: She prefers small gatherings.

5. Use active rather than passive voice whenever possible.
Active voice is more dynamic and usually more concise
than passive voice.

Passive: It is believed by the elders that wisdom will
    prevail.
Active: The elders believe that wisdom will prevail.

6. Avoid the progressive tense when possible; use the present
tense instead.

Progressive: I am wondering what this means.
Present: I wonder what this means.

Progressive: You will be finding that your messages
    are clearer.
Present: You will find that your messages are clearer.

Examples of How to Rewrite Passive, Vague Phrases to Make Them Active and Specific

Passive, Vague: It was determined that . . .
Active, Specific: The committee found that . . .

Passive: It is stated in the report that . . .
Active: The report states that. . .

Passive, Vague: It has been decided that . . .
Active, Specific: The CEO decided that . . .

Passive: It would be appreciated if . . .
Active: Please . . .

Passive: He was not heard by anyone.
Active: No one heard him.

Passive, Vague: It was felt that the report was too
    long.
Active, Specific: Mary thought the report was three
    pages too long.

Vague: Somewhat behind schedule . . .
Specific: One week late . . .

Vague: Very overdrawn . . .
Specific: Overdrawn by $200 . . .

Stuffy: Enclosed please find . . .
Direct: Here is the . . .

Passive, Wordy, Stuffy: This is to inform you that the meeting has been postponed.
Active, Concise, Direct: The meeting has been postponed.

Passive, Vague: The bank meeting was well attended.
Active, Specific: Thirty-five prospective depositors attended the meeting.

Passive: The subject of this manual is employee benefits.
Active: This manual describes employee benefits.

Passive: Our guests are given complimentary fruit baskets.
Active: You will find a fruit basket waiting for you in your room.

Passive: Bonds are sold in all of our branches.
Active: You can buy bonds in any of our branches.

Passive, Wordy: Breakfast and dinner are provided to each resident.
Active, Concise: Residents receive breakfast and dinner.

Passive: It is not a good idea to use vague words such as *very* and *somewhat*.
Active: Be specific; avoid vague words such as *very* and *somewhat*.

Passive, Wordy: Forms of the verb *to be* combined
with the past participle of the main verb are
generally passive. Try not to use them.
Active, Concise: Avoid passive forms of the verb *to
be* when possible.

Passive: *Is* is a weak word.
Active: *Is* weakens a sentence.

Passive: Beth is a good writer.
Active: Beth writes well.

Passive, Wordy: We'd like to take this opportunity
to tell you how life insurance can benefit you
while you're living.
Active, Direct: How can life insurance help you live
longer?

Wordy: If you take the time to enter our contest,
you might win a million dollars.
Direct: What would you do with a million dollars?

Using Words Correctly
• as far as X is concerned; as for X

Those two constructions are different. *As far as* should not
be used in place of the prepositional phrase *as for.* When
you say "as far as," you must follow it with a subject and a
verb.

Wrong: As far as the weather, it doesn't matter if it
rains. (The subject *weather* has no verb; it needs a
verb.)

Correct: As far as the weather is concerned, it
doesn't matter if it rains. (The subject is *weather;*
the verb, *is concerned*.)

If you use the prepositional phrase *as for,* then you don't
need a verb, just an object.

As for the weather, it doesn't matter if it rains.

As for Brian, he wore a raincoat.

• because; as; since

These three words are not interchangeable. If they are used
incorrectly, they can cause confusion and misunderstanding.
Both *since* and *as* can relate to time as well as to cause;
therefore using them to show causal relations can lead to
ambiguity. For example, how would you interpret the next
sentence?

As I spoke to the group, she walked out.

Did she walk out *because* I spoke to the group or did she just
happen to walk out *while* I was speaking?

And what does *Since* mean in the following sentence?

Since the company moved its headquarters,
suppliers were changed.

Did the company change suppliers *because* it moved, or did
they just happen to have been changed *after* the move?

Sometimes the safest way to show a causal relationship is
to use the unambiguous word *because.* And yes, you can
start a sentence with *because.*

Because profits fell, prices rose.

• capitalization

Business writing suffers from overcapitalization. The only time a person's title needs to be capitalized is when it immediately precedes the person's name and is part of the name. Organizations, administrations, boards, and other groups do not need to be capitalized except when their whole official names are used. Correct examples:

> President Lincoln was tall.
> The tall man resembled President Lincoln.
> Abraham Lincoln, president of the United States
>   during the Civil War, was a tall man.
> The president and his wife went to the theater.
> The board of directors met in the president's office.
> The vice president was absent; the chairman
>   presided; and the board voted.
> The treasurer's report prompted discussion.
> She wanted a seat on the board of education.
> He stood in line at the post office and then paid a
>   fine at traffic court.

• comparisons

Comparisons are a matter of degree: much, more, most; good, better, best; poor, poorer, poorest; friendly, friendlier, friendliest. Forming them correctly depends on whether they will be used as adjectives (modifying nouns) or adverbs (modifying verbs, adjectives, or other adverbs); on how many syllables they have; and on arbitrariness.

Some comparative words have the same form whether they're used as adjectives or as adverbs.

> He is the fastest speaker. (*fastest* as adjective)
> He speaks fastest. (*fastest* as adverb)

Certain words cannot be compared because they describe absolute conditions.

Wrong: Her presentation was more unique.
Correct: Her presentation was unique.

Wrong: He offered the most perfect solution.
Correct: He offered the perfect solution.

Many adverbs are formed by adding *ly* to adjectives: *slow, slowly; quiet, quietly; happy, happily.* To use the *ly* adverbs as comparatives, you must use a helper word such as *more, less, most,* or *least,* as in the following correct examples:

John ran more slowly than Bob.
Bob ran less slowly than John.
Sylvia ran most slowly of all.
Stephanie ran least slowly of all.

You can't say "He ran slower than Bob" because *slower* is an adjective, and adjectives do not modify verbs. You must use the comparative adverb *more slowly* to describe the verb *ran*.

• fewer; less
Use *fewer* with things that can be counted or numbered: desks, people; use *less* with nouns that denote mass: water, sand.

His vial contained fewer drops of water. (Drops can be counted.)
Her vial contained less water than his. (Water cannot be counted.)

Not too long ago, Morgan Stanley aired a TV commercial that talked about changes taking place in the financial world. The major point was that at Morgan Stanley, things were "less old," and there were "less boys" in the old boys' club. Ad writers often spurn grammar in their efforts to be clever. In this case, they should have said there were *fewer* boys. The ad would have had just as much punch, and the company would not have risked irritating viewers who care about the rules of language. Business should be innovative with goods and services but not with grammar.

• from A to Z
When you use the word *from*, you must also use the word *to*. Do not substitute a dash or hyphen for the word *to*.

> Wrong: The seminar will run from Aug. 5-Aug. 9.
> Correct: The seminar will run from Aug. 5 to Aug. 9.

> Wrong: The meeting lasted from nine-noon or from
> 9-12.
> Correct: The meeting lasted from nine to noon or
> from 9 to 12.

• good, well; bad, badly
Good and *bad* are adjectives; they modify nouns. *Well* and *badly* are adverbs; they modify verbs, adjectives, and other adverbs. In the next sentence, the verb *smelled* refers to a state of being, so it is followed by the adjective *good*, which describes Toby.

> Toby smelled good because he had just taken a
> shower.

But in the following sentence, *smelled* is an action verb modified by the adverb *well*, which describes how capably Toby performed the action of smelling.

> Toby smelled well after surgery to remove the
> blockage in his nose.

If you are healthy, you may say:
> I feel good.

If your fingers are extremely sensitive, you may say:
> I feel well.

If you are sick, you may say:
> I feel bad.

If you are sorry for something you did, you may say:
> I feel badly.

• impact

Impact is a noun that careful writers do not use as a verb. If you want to use a verb that means "have an impact on," say *affect*. The only thing that should be impacted is a tooth.

> Wrong: Her decision impacted the workplace.
> Correct: Her decision had an impact on the
> workplace.
> Correct: Her decision affected the workplace.
> Correct: He reeled from the impact.

• like; as; as if

Like should not be followed by a noun and verb but just by a noun, pronoun, or noun phrase. *Like* does not mean "the way" or "as if."

> Wrong: He talks like I do.
> Correct: He talks the way I do.
> Correct: He talks as I do.

> Wrong: Sally closed this sale like she closed the last one.
> Correct: Sally closed this sale the way she closed the last one.

> Wrong: It seems like she said it correctly.
> Correct: It seems as if she said it correctly.

> Correct: Like the other pedestrians, she waited for a break in traffic.
> Correct: They go together like peas and carrots.
> Correct: It fits like a glove.

• myself

The pronoun *myself* should be used reflexively or intensively. It almost always refers to the subject of the sentence. It should not be used as a substitute for the pronoun *me*.

> Wrong: Dozens of people, including Stuart and myself, plan to attend the opening.
> Correct: Dozens of people, including Stuart and me, plan to attend the opening.

> Wrong: He is a workaholic like myself.
> Correct: He is a workaholic like me.

> Wrong: Please tell Cheryl and myself when you're
>   ready.
> Correct: Please tell Cheryl and me when you're
>   ready.

When *myself* is the object of a verb or preposition, it is called reflexive. When it is used for emphasis, it is called intensive. In the following examples, *myself* is used correctly.

> I want to do it myself.
> Let me see for myself.
> I myself ordered the parts.
> I'm going to work by myself.
> Myself, I don't care.

* quotation marks
Unnecessary use of quotation marks makes writing look childish. Four situations require the use of quotation marks:

(1) When you quote something said or written.
> The chairman said, "Please come to order."

(2) When you refer to words as words.
> The word "quality" is often used incorrectly as an
>   adjective.

(3) When you introduce a new word.
> I'm going to call him a "blad." A blad is a bad lad.
>   (Notice that quotation marks are not needed the
>   second time the word is used.)

(4) When you cite a magazine article or song title.
> Her article "Walking to China" appeared in a travel
>   magazine.

• there's; there are

There's only one definition of *there's:* it is a contraction of *there is* or *there has.* And *is* and *has* are singular verbs. When referring to more than one person or thing, use *there are.*

> Wrong: There's a dozen ways to solve the problem.
> Correct: There are a dozen ways to solve the
>   problem.

> Wrong: There's many good answers to that
>   question.
> Correct: There are many good answers to that
>   question.

> Correct: There's only one way to solve that problem.
> Correct: There's a good answer to that question.
> Correct: There's no microphone for the speaker.
> Correct: There's been no solution. (There has been)
> Correct: There are several topics on the agenda.
> Correct: There are three phones on his desk.

• used to

Use the past tense, *used,* when combining it with an infinitive to describe something in the past.

> Sheila used to drive to work, but now she takes
>   rapid transit.
> The programs used to be compatible.

But there's an exception. (Isn't there always an exception?) When the phrase includes *did* or *didn't,* then *use to* is correct.

> Sheila did use to drive to work.
> The programs didn't use to be compatible.

• who; that
When referring to people, use *who.*

> The applicant who won the post was pleased.
> Fred, who walked in first, sat at the head of the
>   table.

When referring to anything other than people, use *that* or *which.*

> The company that ran the ad was inundated with
>   applicants.
> The table, which was made of oak, accommodated
>   twelve.

Choosing the Right Word
• affect – effect
Both words can be used as both nouns and verbs. But most often, *affect* is used as a verb meaning "to influence or have an effect on."

> The new rule affected his behavior.

And most often, *effect* is used as a noun meaning "result or influence."

> The new rule had an effect on his behavior.

In psychology, *affect* is used as a noun meaning "emotion."

> Medication dulled his affect.

The verb *effect* means "to bring about."

> Management effected change through new rules.

• it's – its
If you mean to say *it is*, then use the contraction *it's*.

>It's going to be a short meeting.

If you want to show possession, then use the possessive
pronoun *its*.

>The group used its clout to get better
>accommodations.

• lie – lay
Chickens lay eggs. People and dogs lie down. It's easy to get
confused because *lay* is also the past tense of *lie*.
For the present, say:

>Now please lay the book on the desk.
>Now you may lay yourself down.
>I can't seem to lay my hands on the receipt.
>The comedian is laying an egg.

For the past, say:

>Yesterday you lay down to take a nap.
>Last night the cat lay on my bed.
>Yesterday you laid the book on the desk.
>He laid his hands on the report just in time.
>Chickens laid eggs.
>The chickens had laid their eggs before breakfast.

Lay is a transitive verb, which means it must be followed by
a direct object. You must lay *something* (the direct object)
down. In the sentence *Now I lay me down to sleep*, the direct
object of *lay* is *me*. In the sentence *Lay the napkins on the
table*, the direct object of *Lay* is *napkins*.

Lie is an intransitive verb, which means it cannot be followed by a direct object. Correctly say:

> Please lie down and make yourself comfortable.
> She was lying down when the phone rang.
> The dog was lying in the grass.
> He lay awake for hours.
> They had lain down on the job.

• parameter – perimeter

Good writers don't use *parameter* when they mean *perimeter*. *Perimeter* means *boundary*. *Parameter* is a mathematical term that should be used only by people who understand its technical meaning; it doesn't belong in most business writing; it doesn't mean *guideline* or *limit* or *scope*.

• your – you're

Even if you're one of those people who pronounce *your* and *you're* so that they sound the same, your common sense should tell you when to use which word in writing.

Your is a possessive pronoun.

> Your side is different from his

You're is a contraction for the pronoun and verb *you are*.

> You're on the right side.

References

The American Heritage Book of English Usage. Boston: Houghton Mifflin Company, 1996.

The American Heritage Dictionary of the English Language. 3rd ed. Boston: Houghton Mifflin, 1996.

Baron, Naomi S. *Alphabet to Email: How Written English Evolved and Where It's Heading*. New York: Routledge, 2000.

Cavanagh, Christina A. *Email in the Workplace: Discovering Unproductive Practices*. The University of Western Ontario, September 2001.

The Chicago Manual of Style. 14th ed. Chicago: University of Chicago Press, 1993.

Dumond, Val. *Grammar for Grownups*. New York: HarperCollins, 1993.

Eggenschwiler, Jean. *Writing: Grammar, Usage, and Style*. Lincoln, NE: Cliffs Notes, 1997.

E-What? A Guide to the Quirks of New Media Style and Usage. By the editors of EEI Press. Alexandria, VA: EEI Press, 2000.

Garner, Bryan A. *A Dictionary of Modern American Usage.* New York: Oxford University Press, 1998.

Johnson, Edward D. *The Handbook of Good English.* New York: Washington Square Press, 1991.

Lederer, Richard and Richard Dowis. *Sleeping Dogs Don't Lay: Practical Advice for the Grammatically Challenged.* New York: St. Martin's Press, 1999.

McCutcheon, Marc. *Roget's Superthesaurus.* 2nd ed. Cincinnati: Writer's Digest Books, 1998.

Merriam-Webster's Dictionary of Synonyms. Springfield, MA: Merriam-Webster, 1993.

The New York Times Manual of Style and Usage. Edited by Allan M. Siegal and William G. Connolly. New York: Random House, 1999.

Strunk, William, Jr., and E. B. White. *The Elements of Style.* 4th ed. Boston: Allyn & Bacon, 1999.

Webster's New World College Dictionary. 4th ed. New York: Macmillan, 1999.

Index

Acknowledgments

Immeasurable gratitude goes to all those unnamed business correspondents who unknowingly provided examples of errors in formatting and grammar in their e-mail messages, and inspired me to write this book.

I am also grateful to Dinni Gordon, Judith Lopez, and George Mansfield, who read the entire manuscript and offered invaluable suggestions. Judith also allowed me to use sentences from her book, *Immune Dysfunction*, as correct examples.

Thanks to Ruth Kizner, Jeanne Lese, and Chris Van Deusen, who read sections of the first draft and suggested improvements.

For participating in my survey about various e-mail programs and helping me test them, thanks go to Marguerite Couvillion, Ann Munger, Rob Roehrick, Kay Slagle, Barbie Smith, Paul Van Deusen, and others.

For responding to my survey about e-mail pet peeves, I thank Kathy Fitzgerald Sherman, Rick Young, and the following members of Copyediting-L: Andrea Balinson, Sarah Bane, Erika Buky, Brida Connolly, Carol Eastman, Joyce Fetterman, Fran Henry, Willard Hughes, Roger Jones, Linda Kerby, Joy Matkowski, Brenda Mercer, Rhana Pike, Sonya Plowman, Jody Roes, Vicki Rosenzweig, Susan Squires, Ruth E. Thaler-Carter, Pam Wood, Kelly Wright, and Andrea Zuercher. And I'm grateful to three other Copyediting-L members for their contributions: Bill Blinn, Mark L. Levinson, and Joanne Sandstrom. Robert Goodman, Rick Kamen, and Sara Terrien also deserve thanks.

Finally, to Hal Smith (no relation), for his editorial suggestions, encouragement, and support: thank you.

About the author

Lisa A. Smith is an award-winning writer of training and business communications, an editor with more than 25 years of experience, and a presenter of seminars on business writing and marketing communications. Her educational materials have won a Christopher Award, first place in the American Journal of Nursing Media Festival competition, a Silver Screen Award from the U.S. Industrial Film Festival, and a Gold Cindy Award from the Information Film Producers of America.

Interior Fonts
Goudy Old Style, Goudy Sans Lt, Goudy SC

Cover Design
by
Rob Roehrick, www.roehrickdesign.com

Special Sales

Discounts are available from the publisher on bulk orders for special markets or premium use.

On large orders, a message from your company or organization may be printed in the book.

Individuals may also order directly from the publisher.

For more information, please contact:

Special Markets Department
Writing & Editing at Work
PO Box 2543, San Anselmo, CA 94979

admin@writingandeditingatwork.com